MARRAKESH, EXPLORE THE MAGIC OF THE RED CITY

An insider's guide to the best places to eat, drink and explore

YASMIN ZEINAB

Photography by
ALISTAIR WHEELER

T0322536

Hardie Grant

TRAVEL

Welcome to Marrakesh

There is truly no other place in the world quite like Marrakesh. It is a dizzying city full of contradictions: it moves fast and slow, its rapid beat and frenzied streets are juxtaposed by scenes of Marrakeshis lingering over mint tea and indulging in streetside conversation for hours. It is both open and mysterious: much is in plain sight but dig a little deeper and you'll find the real beauty of the city hidden behind towering walls and unmarked doors, and embedded in the essence of its people and culture. It is both ancient and modern: the city is anchored in the past, with its historical sights and centuries-old traditions, but it looks to the future in many ways, like with its flourishing contemporary art and design scene. Marrakesh is a bewildering and mysterious place but it is all part of its magic.

I am not Moroccan but I have always felt at home in Marrakesh. Since my first visit many years ago, I have been spellbound by the chaotic rhythm of the city, its vivid beauty, captivating culture and knack for adventure. Each time I return, my fascination with Marrakesh only deepens. It is a city that lets me speak a jumble of Arabic, English and French, and speaks back to me in the same way. Marrakesh welcomes all as they are, with its famed hospitality.

More so than other cities, Marrakesh has many versions of itself. Whether you are a seasoned visitor of the Red City or a first-timer, my hope is to introduce you to my version of Marrakesh. The places in this book are a tightly curated collection of venues that each represent the city in their own way. But my hope is also that you will use this book to discover your own version of Marrakesh. The version that I cannot show you; that no book can. It exists in the spirit of the city, in its colours, in its sounds and in the warmth of its people.

Yasmin

About
Marrakesh

Marrakesh is a bustling city of exotic charm, steeped in history, where old and new converge at every corner. The first of Morocco's four imperial cities, Marrakesh, nicknamed the Red City for its dusty terracotta coloured walls, has a long and complex history.

Built, destroyed, reconstructed and demolished throughout protracted power struggles between Berber tribes, dynasties, vast empires and colonial forces, Marrakesh's colourful past has shaped the diverse and rich city we know today. Founded by the Almoravid dynasty in 1062, the Almohads seized the city from them in 1147 and held power for many centuries. The savvy Saadian dynasty took over in the 16th century, until they fell a century later to the powerful Alaouites. In 1912, the French Protectorate took control of the country, until Morocco's independence in 1956 saw the restoration of the Alaouites as the country's monarchs. Each of these rulers left their distinct mark on Marrakesh: they built sophisticated infrastructure, beautiful mosques, opulent palaces and grand gardens, many of which still stand as extraordinary examples of Moroccan architecture and artisanship.

Marrakesh is an incredibly multicultural place, with African, Arab, Berber and French influences, yet Moroccan traditions and culture and, above all, the abundant hospitality of Marrakeshis, remain at its core. The fabled trails of nomads and traders of ancient Marrakesh have given way to some modernisation, but its exotica and mesmerising souks (markets) continue to seduce travellers. In recent years, it has become a destination for contemporary African art and design, and a breeding ground for savvy entrepreneurs and talented creatives. Marrakesh is a complex city with many faces, each as dazzling as the next. It is glamourous, romantic, rough, alluring, calm and chaotic, all at the same time, and there is adventure to be found at every turn.

About

DO & DON'T

A sensory overload of rich colours, frenzied sounds and fragrant scents, Marrakesh is an intoxicating city. It is bursting with life and opportunity for adventure; however, Marrakesh can frazzle even the most seasoned travellers. Here's a list of dos and don'ts to help you navigate the Red City.

DO take the time to understand the city and its way of life. Unlike many other cities, Marrakesh will open up to you quickly if you take the time to understand them. The best way to do this is by speaking to the locals who will happily oblige, Marrakeshis are great conversationalists.

DO accept mint tea whenever it is offered to you. At the heart of Moroccan hospitality, mint tea is offered at almost all social encounters.

DO have at least one hammam. An ancient bathing ritual, it is the ultimate Moroccan experience. See the Relax chapter (see p.135 and p.171) for more information.

DO make an effort to learn some basic Arabic. While most people you encounter will speak English, knowing how to say hello, goodbye and thank you in the local language is always appreciated. Ask a local how best to pronounce these greetings.

DO dress modestly. Both Moroccan men and women tend to dress conservatively so follow suit and opt for below-the-knee hemlines and covered shoulders.

DO stay in the medina. There is no area more authentic in which to sleep. The medina's winding maze-like alleys are full of riads (traditional houses) that have been converted into charming guesthouses and luxury boutique hotels. See the Stay chapter (see p.143) for more information.

DO shop beyond the souks. An enticing collection of vibrant marketplaces full of traditional artisans and traders, shopping in the souks is a must (see p.107), but don't limit your experience there. Be sure to browse the stores in the winding alleys around these marketplaces, and in Marrakesh's industrial area–turned design hub, Sidi Ghanem, as in them you'll find unique pieces and discover some of Marrakesh's established and up-and-coming talent. See the Shop chapter (see p.107) for more information.

DO eat the street food. It is a well-known fact that the best Moroccan food is found at home, but it is also found in the street. Join the locals at streetside food stands and hole-in-the-wall eateries for some of the best food in Marrakesh. See the Street Food chapter (see p.59) for more information.

DO prepare to be firm with taxi drivers. Despite being asked, drivers will rarely turn on their meter. If they don't, don't negotiate on price but pay the unspoken but universally agreed price rates. See p.167 for more information.

DO download an offline map, such as maps.me. Phone reception can be patchy at the best of times in the medina so don't rely on data to get you around. See p.173 for more information.

DO be on alert for pickpockets.

DON'T be in a rush. Marrakesh runs on its own time. Surrender to the city and its way of life. Make plans but not too many, as Marrakesh has its way of changing them. Wandering the medina without agenda or destination is the ultimate way to experience the city.

DON'T leave the airport without cash if you haven't arranged a pre-paid transfer. See p.172 for more information.

DON'T take photos of the snake charmers and performers in Jemaa el-Fnaa (see p.71) without being prepared to pay. If the performers see you taking photos, they will approach you for money. Don't be intimidated into overpaying. Small change is sufficient.

DON'T listen to unsolicited advice from strangers in the medina. It is a pastime of young boys to mislead tourists with false directions or misinformation. See p.171 for more information.

DON'T get too worked up about the hecklers and touts. They are harmless, and engaging with them only fuels the fire, so it's best to ignore them. See p.171 for more information.

DON'T accept a chaperone if you get lost, unless you are prepared to pay for the help. See p.171 for more information.

DON'T drink the tap water. See p.170 for more information.

Do and Don't

Marrakesh

Key

1. Berber Museum
   and Jardin Majorelle
2. Medersa Ben Youssef
3. Koutoubia Mosque
4. Jemaa el-Fnaa
5. Bahia Palace
6. Saadian Tombs

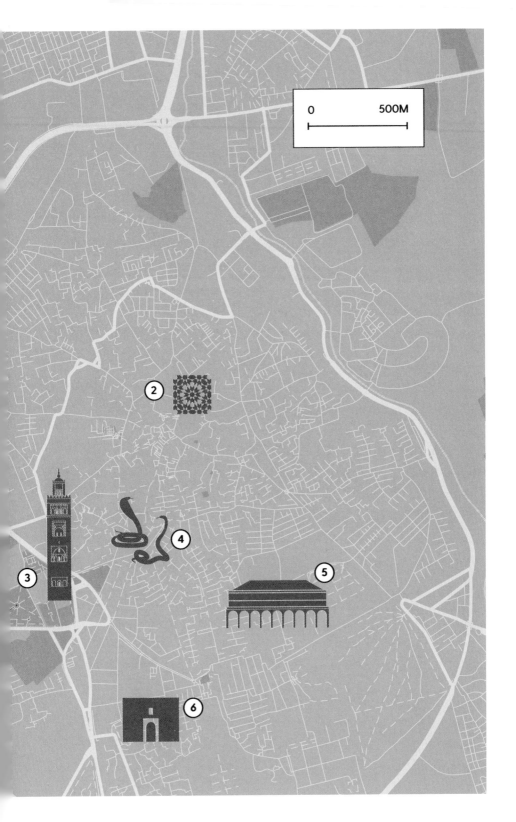

NEIGHBOURHOOD INDEX

Notable Neighbourhoods

Marrakesh has two distinct areas: the ancient city – the medina, ringed within centuries-old ramparts; and Guéliz/ Ville Nouvelle – the modern, planned part of the city found outside the medina's historic walls. The medina is dizzying, with a labyrinthine layout and a honeycomb network of diverse neighbourhoods that makes getting lost inevitable. Here is an overview of Marrakesh's key areas to help you get your bearings.

MEDINA

At the core of the Red City is the ancient arrowhead-shaped medina. Enclosed by 19 kilometres (12 miles) of towering, centuries-old terracotta coloured pisé (rammed earth) ramparts built by the Almohad dynasty in the 12th century, the medina is accessible by one of 19 historic babs (gates), each functioning as a unique reference point to distinct neighbourhoods. At the heart of the medina, in the shadow of the iconic minaret of the Koutoubia Mosque (see p.87), is Jemaa el-Fnaa (see p.71), the city's famed square. Part of the UNESCO World Heritage Site with action in every direction – snake charmers, fortune tellers, musicians, henna artists, slapstick performers and persistent touts – Jemaa el-Fnaa is a feast for the senses. All winding paths that make up the maze of the medina eventually lead back to the square and you'll return to it countless times as you navigate this part of Marrakesh.

North of Jemaa el-Fnaa lay the mesmerising souks (see p.107), countless restaurants (see Eat and Drink chapter, p.31), hammams (see Relax chapter, p.135) and many of Marrakesh's key cultural attractions (see Explore chapter, p.69) that form the centre of the medina. Further north, east and west, rung around the central core of the medina are snaking alleys that make up the more residential areas, where urban life takes place in an ancient setting. Many of the city's riads are here: beautiful courtyard homes

Neighbourhoods

converted into guesthouses and boutique hotels, where you can be immersed in the fusion of contemporary and traditional design (see Stay chapter, p.143). These neighbourhoods offer a glimpse of everyday life: Marrakeshis picking up bread from bakeries, collecting produce at frenzied local markets, kids playing soccer in narrow alleys and wizened men socialising over mint tea on streetside corners.

KASBAH

In the south of the medina is the ancient royal area, the kasbah. Its Qur'anic inscribed gate, Bab Agnaou, is one of the most impressive and celebrated of the medina's 19 babs (gates). Once home to powerful figures, sultans and ruthless rulers, there are opulent mansions, grand architecture and the remains of royal places dotted throughout the kasbah. Nestled between El Badi Palace (see p.91) and Bahia Palace (see p.93) is the Mellah, the former Jewish quarter. Established in the 15th century, key monuments include the synagogue and the Miara cemetery, the largest Jewish cemetery in Morocco, which remain significant today.

GUÉLIZ/VILLE NOUVELLE

When the French Protectorate began in 1912, the French set about the urban expansion of Marrakesh. French army general Hubert Lyautey, the first resident of the French Protectorate, had grand plans for infrastructure developments. However, he also wanted to conserve the heritage of Marrakesh, so he enlisted Henri Prost, a French architect and urban planner, to create a new city – a Ville Nouvelle – outside the ancient medina walls. The neighbourhood of Guéliz was a hub of the French Protectorate, housing government buildings and colonial businesses until Morocco's independence from the French in 1956. Today Guéliz/Ville Nouvelle is a hotspot of art and culture: the Art Deco buildings have been converted into contemporary art galleries, such as Comptoir des Mines (see p.103), and former colonial outposts have been turned into trendy eateries, such as Grand Café de la Poste (see p.52).

NOTABLE NEIGHBOURHOODS

HIVERNAGE

In 1928, Hubert Lyautey and Henri Prost began the development of a more exclusive neighbourhood for French diplomats and government officials, which quickly became a destination for the elite in search of winter sun. In 1929, together with French architect Antoine Marchisio, Prost built the legendary hotel, La Mamounia (see p.141) in the heart of the Hivernage. A beacon of luxury and a Marrakesh institution, it set the tone for the hotels that would follow in its wake. The Hivernage has long been a playground for celebrities, attachés and jet-setters, and its wide palm tree-lined avenues remain a hub of luxury hotels, upscale restaurants and nightlife establishments, such as Comptoir Darna (see p.55).

SIDI GHANEM

Four kilometres (two and a half miles) north-west of the medina, Marrakesh's industrial area, Sidi Ghanem, once a barren part of the city and home only to warehouses, has emerged as a shopping mecca. Its appeal is due in large part to a new generation of creatives who have flocked to the Red City, establishing thriving businesses that merge the savoir-faire (know-how) of Moroccan artisans with contemporary design. Showrooms and ateliers such as Marrakshi Life (see p.129) and LRNCE (see p.133) have championed Sidi Ghanem's transformation into a hub for design.

PALMERAIE

East of the city, approximately 10 kilometres (6 miles) from the medina, lies the Palmeraie, an endless palm tree grove. As legend has it, this vast expanse came to be when, in the 11th century, Almoravid Sultan Yussef Ben Tachefine and his entourage littered date seeds across the plains, while in search of land for his dynasty, leading to the sprouting of thousands of towering palms. A green oasis, the Palmeraie is dotted with luxury resorts, grand villas and unique properties, such as Dar Sadaka (see p.157) and is the destination of choice for luxury travellers looking to relax poolside away from the chaotic medina.

MEDINA EXPLORING

FULL-DAY ITINERARY

Marrakesh's long and rich history has left a legacy of opulent palaces, stunning mosques and impressive infrastructure. Make sure to book ahead for a hammam at Farnatchi Spa and to reserve a spot at Comptoir Darna.

9AM Ease into a full day of sightseeing with a coffee or a mint tea at ① **Zeitoun Café**. On a lively corner of the Kasbah, directly across from the Saadian Tombs (the next stop), the cafe's street-side terrace is a great place to soak up the neighbourhood. Most hotels and riads (a traditional Moroccan courtyard house) offer breakfast to their guests, however Zeitoun Café also does a decent Moroccan breakfast of staples like m'semen (a Moroccan pancake) and eggs.

9.30AM Once you're caffeinated, cross the street and veer right to find the entrance of the ② **Saadian Tombs** (see p.89), the opulent burial site of sultans of the Saadian dynasty that ruled Morocco from 1549 to 1659. Visit the Chamber of 12 Pillars, the tomb of sultan Ahmad al-Mansur, decorated with a mosaic floor, a finely crafted cedar ceiling and towering Carrara marble pillars.

10.30AM On leaving the tombs to reach the next stop, ③ **El Badi Palace** (see p.91), walk back towards Zeitoun Café, follow the road and then take a right at the end of the street (marked by an archway). Follow the street until you reach a T-intersection, turn left and then immediately right. Follow the road, turn right at the roundabout, then right after the arch and the entrance to the palace will be on your right. The walk should take no more than 10 minutes. Built by Saadian sultan Ahmad al-Mansur in the 16th century, today only the palace foundations remain but you'll get a sense of the extraordinary place it must have been.

11.30AM A 10-minute walk north-east will take you to ④ **Bahia Palace** (see p.93). From El Badi Palace, exit the way you came in, retrace your steps to the roundabout, take the first exit and follow the road for a few minutes until you reach the entrance to Bahia Palace. A vast complex commissioned towards the end of the 19th century by the then Grand Vizer Si Moussa, Bahia Palace has lush gardens, incredible traditional zellige (mosaic tiles) and intricate zouak (painted wood) ceilings.

12.30PM Next onto lunch to refuel and rest your weary feet. From the palace, follow your steps back down the windy path towards the roundabout. After 450 metres (0.28 miles), take a right and continue straight for a few minutes and you'll find yourself on Rue Riad Zitoun el Jedid, a key vein of the medina that eventually leads to Jemaa el-Fnaa. The lane presents two options for lunch. The first: (5) **La Famille** (see p.41) is a coveted vegetarian restaurant-cum-boutique that offers three changing options for a light lunch. Or continue for 150 metres (492 feet) to (6) **Naranj** (see p.43), the city's go-to spot for Lebanese food (also vegetarian friendly); ask for a table on the rooftop terrace.

2PM After lunch, head to (7) **Musée de la Femme** (see p.81), dedicated to exhibitions on the role of Moroccan women in the country's social and political landscape. Turn right out of your chosen restaurant and follow the street until you reach a fork in the road; veer left and follow the road until you reach a T-intersection. Turn left, follow the road round and then take the first left and then the second right turn until you reach another T-intersection. Take a right and then a left and you'll find the museum after a few minutes on your right.

3PM Take a five-minute walk to (8) **Medersa Ben Youssef** (see p.77), a former Islamic school. To get here from the museum, turn left and then right, follow the path for a few minutes, take the next right, then immediately turn left. Follow the street until the next available right, take the turn and arrive at the entrance. Medersa Ben Youssef has a humble facade but inside it transforms into an ornate space. Around the courtyard, a pattern of zellige (mosaic tiles) in blues and greens meets dusty orange stucco and intricate cedar woodwork.

4PM End a busy day with a hammam (traditional Moroccan bath) at (9) **Farnatchi Spa** (see p.138, you'll need to book ahead), just minutes away from Medersa Ben Youssef. Turn right and walk to the end of the street and take a right at the T-intersection. After approximately 50 metres (164 feet) you'll see the spa's discreet door on your left. Opt for the classic hammam and relax before retiring to your accommodation for downtime before the evening.

7PM Start the night out with a drink on the rooftop at (10) **El Fenn Bar** (see p.44). The bar is just minutes from Jemaa el-Fnaa (see p.71) and offers enviable views of the medina and the Atlas Mountains. Pull up a seat at the oak bar and order from a list of classic cocktails.

9PM Next, onto a Moroccan dinner at (11) **Comptoir Darna** (see p.55). From El Fenn, turn left and left again to get back to the main street to hail a taxi. Comptoir Darna is the go-to for dinner with a show, and at 10pm each night, a band of belly-dancers twirl around the restaurant. The food can be hit-and-miss, but it is a must-do Marrakesh experience for first-timers. Reservations are required.

MEDINA SHOPPING & EATING

FULL-DAY ITINERARY

Spend a day exploring the enticing souks and the independent boutique stores opened by a new generation of creatives, who are combining ancient Moroccan craftsmanship with a modern outlook. Between shopping, you can rest in a garden and eat beautiful local food. Be sure to make a reservation at Nomad in advance.

11AM Start your shopping at ① **Laly** (see p.119) in south medina, a beautiful label offering colourful flowing dresses and loose-fitting garments in luxurious lightweight fabrics.

11.30AM From Laly, turn left and follow the road for approximately 200 metres (656 feet) until the next left. Turn and follow the road for another 300 metres (984 feet) until you arrive at ② **Malakut** (see p.108), a tiny store with unique ceramics and a small line of contemporary Moroccan clothing, all handmade in Marrakesh.

12PM On the opposite side of the street just two stores down is ③ **Kitan** (see p.114), a charming clothing boutique where Japanese design meets Moroccan craftsmanship.

12.30PM On leaving Kitan, turn right and follow the path for a minute or so until you reach a fork in the road. Veer right and keep an eye out on your right-hand side for the clearly-marked entrance to ④ **Max & Jan** (see p.111), a sprawling hub of contemporary clothing, accessories and homewares.

1PM Next, onto lunch at ⑤ **Chez Lamine** (see p.61), just off Jemaa el-Fnaa (see p.71). To get here from Max & Jan, take a left and retrace your steps from this morning, following the street past Kitan and Malakut until you reach a T-intersection. Take a right, the next left, then the second right, and follow the street until you reach another T-intersection. Take a left and then follow the street until you see stalls selling fresh mint and other herbs, take a right and you'll find yourself amongst a row of stalls forming what is known as Mechoui Alley. Each stall sells mechoui: whole lamb slow-roasted for several hours in underground clay pits. At Chez Lamine, the roast lambs are carved-up, sprinkled with cumin and salt, and served with hot bread and mint tea.

2PM Walk off lunch by immersing yourself in the ⑥ **Souk** (see p.73) for the afternoon. To enter, from Chez Lamine take a left and then the next alley that appears on your right. The souk is a collection of vibrant marketplaces, organised by a particular product or trade. For the best experience wander freely and don't worry if you get lost in the winding alleys.

4PM Once you're done with shopping, from the souk, follow signs for ⑦ **Place des Épices** (the Spice Market, see p.75). Once there, use Café des Épices as your point of reference. Cross the square, walking west (keep Café des Épices on you left) until you reach a T-intersection. Take a left and then the first right through an archway, you'll see a small black and white sign for ⑧ **Shtatto** (see p.38). Head to the rooftop – a mutli-tiered space showcasing Moroccan artists and designers – and sink into the green lounges and enjoy the sweeping views with a mint tea. Once rested, head back down the stairs, pit-stopping at ⑨ **Nasire** (see p.109) on level 2 to admire the beautifully handcrafted leather bags and on level 1, the designs of coveted Moroccan designer, ⑩ **Amine Bendriouich** (see p.116).

5PM Spend the rest of the afternoon at ⑪ **Le Jardin Secret** (see p.86), a sprawling 16th-century garden with an exotic garden and an Islamic garden. From Shtatto, turn right and follow the street staying to the right, until you reach a T-intersection. Turn left onto Rue Azbezd, and follow the street for a few minutes passing Medersa Ben Youssef, until you reach a fork in the road. Turn left and follow the road, taking a quick right then left at the end of Derb Zaouiat Lahdar to keep going straight onto Rue Amesfah. Follow the street for a few minutes before reaching the garden on your right.

6.30PM Begin your evening at the sprawling and chaotic square of ⑫ **Jemaa el-Fnaa** (see p.71). Turn right out of the gardens, head south along Rue Mouassine, turn right when the road ends, and then take your first left on to Rue Fehl Chidmi, which will take you to the Jemaa el-Fnaa. Join the crowd, soak in the square's magic and be alert for pickpocketing.

7.30PM As the sun begins to set, head to the southern corner of Jemaa el-Fnaa to the top terrace of ⑬ **Café de France** (see p.71), for a mint tea and uninterrupted views of the square.

8:30PM Take a short walk to ⑭ **Nomad** (see p.33) for rooftop dining, with views of the medina and Atlas Mountains. Reservations are essential, ask for a table on the top terrace. To get here from Café de France, walk straight keeping Zeitoun Café on your right. Once you've passed the cafe, take a right, retracing your steps to lunchspot Chez Lamine, pass the foodstall and take a left to enter the souk. Take the next right and follow the path for a few minutes, take the next right; the entrance to Nomad is on your right-hand side. Order from a menu of modern Moroccan and settle in for a night under the stars.

Itinerary

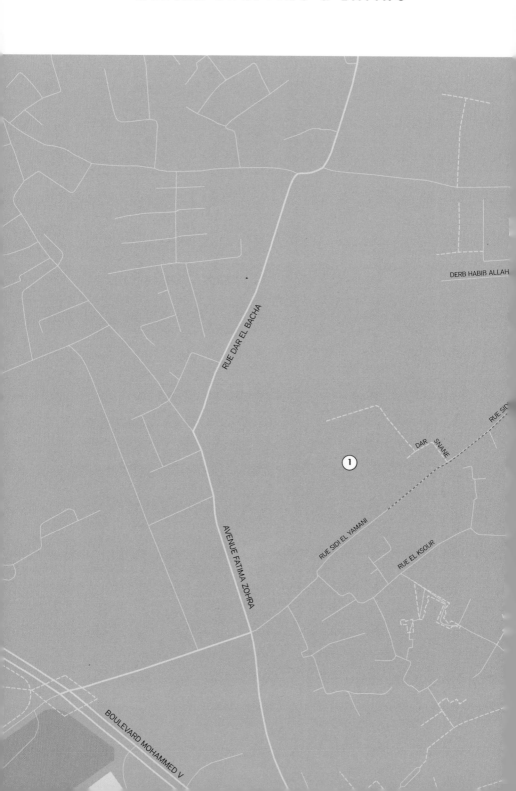

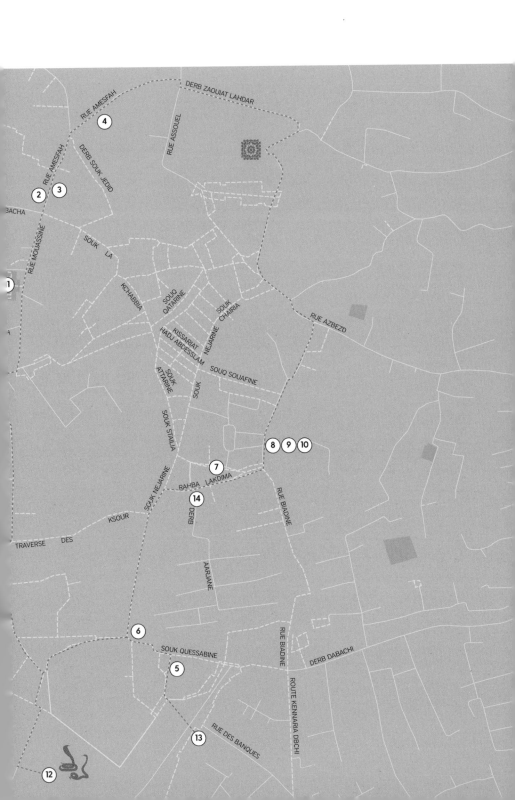

Guéliz/Ville Nouvelle (the new city) was created during the French Protectorate-era, and the French-style wide avenues here are dense with museums, lesser-known art galleries and unique boutiques.

8AM Arrive early to beat the crowds to ① **Jardin Majorelle** (see p.97), a botanical garden and the most-visited sight in Morocco. Buy a combined ticket for entrance to the Berber Museum and Yves Saint Laurent Museum for later in the morning. The garden was created in the 1920s by French Orientalist painter Jacques Majorelle, who filled it with exotic plants and painted it in a striking cobalt blue (now known as Majorelle blue).

9AM Head inside to the ② **Berber Museum** (see p.99), housed on the ground floor of Majorelle's former studio in the heart of Jardin Majorelle. The museum houses Imazighen (Berber) artefacts collected by late fashion designer Yves Saint Laurent and his partner, Pierre Bergé.

10AM While inside Jardin Majorelle, have a coffee or mint tea break on ③ **Le Café Majorelle**'s orange tree-lined terrace.

10.30AM Exit the garden, turn left and take a short stroll next door to the ④ **Yves Saint Laurent Museum** (see p.95). The designer's love affair with Marrakesh began in the late 1960s and from then on the city became his creative retreat. Be sure to check out the temporary exhibition space.

12:00PM Head back towards Jardin Majorelle and cross the street to ⑤ **33 Majorelle** (see p.122). One of the few concept stores in Marrakesh, it stocks clothing, accessories and homewares from Moroccan designers.

12.30pm Avoid the taxis outside 33 Majorelle and instead turn left and take a short walk to the main street (Avenue Yacoub El Mansour) to hail a taxi. Pay no more than 30 MAD for the 10-minute drive to ⑥ **Plus 61** (see p.49) for lunch from a fusion menu of Mediterranean, Asian and Middle Eastern flavours.

1.30pm After lunch, enter the building immediately on your left and follow the path to the back left of the same floor to the creative world of ⑦ **Maison ARTC** (see p.125). Handmade with upcycled materials, each piece is one-of-a-kind and makes a great keepsake.

2pm Around the block is ⑧ **MACMA** (see p.102), a private museum exhibiting Orientalist works depicting daily life in Morocco by Western artists of the 19th and early 20th centuries.

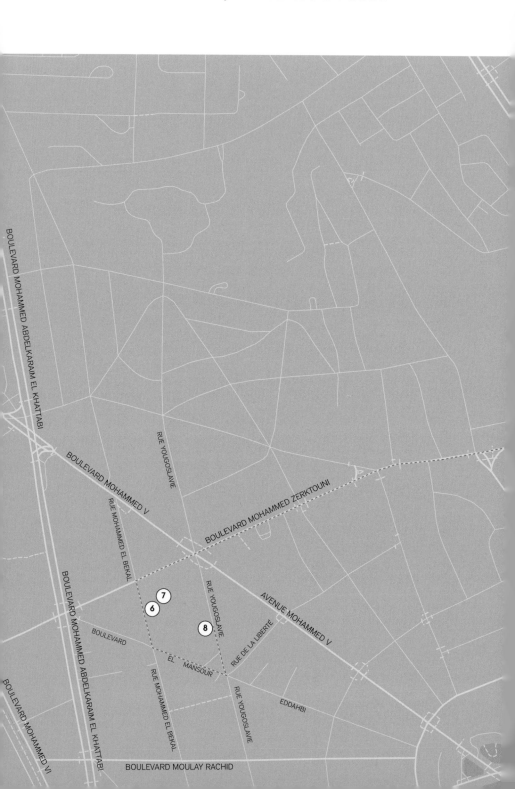

While the souks remain enticing, a new generation of Moroccan and foreign creatives have given traditional artisan techniques a modern approach. Many of their boutiques and ateliers are in Marrakesh's former industrial area, Sidi Ghanem. While each of these showrooms are within 20 minutes' walking distance from each other, they are not on scenic routes, so organising a taxi for the morning is highly recommended. Depending on your negotiation skills, this will cost around 300 MAD.

9AM Start your day at the atelier and showroom of cult label, ① **Marrakshi Life** (see p.129), with its beautiful handmade fabrics and a collection of easy-to-wear pieces.

10AM Approximately a 10-minute drive from Marrakshi Life, turn right onto Rue Sidi Ghanem, take the first left and then the first exit at the roundabout to coveted lifestyle brand, ② **LRNCE** (see p.133). It is located on your right-hand side towards the end of the street on the second floor of an unassuming building, marked only with a very discreet sign. Browse the bright and airy space, full of unique ceramics.

11AM From LRNCE, retrace your route to the roundabout, take the second exit continuing straight on the same street. At the second roundabout, take the first exit to ③ **Le Magasin Général** (see p.131), which is on the second corner on your left-hand side. This store has a collection of 20th-century furniture, and a small range of vintage dainty glassware, candles and French linen.

11.30AM When leaving the store, take a right turn and walk 20 metres (66 feet) until you reach the intersection, take another right and follow the road for 30 metres (98 feet). On your right you'll find the flagship store of the eccentric label ④ **Topolina** (see p.130), well-known for its bold colours, clashing prints and flowing pieces, all handmade in Marrakesh.

12PM From Topolina, take a quick two-minute drive to get to ceramicists ⑤ **Chabi Chic** (see p.127). Continuing on the same street as Topolina, take the first exit at the next roundabout and towards the end of the road on the right-hand side of the street you'll find the warehouse-like space, stacked high with vases, bowls, plates and cups, handpainted in pastel patterns.

1PM Finish your morning's shopping with a 10-minute drive to Guéliz/Ville Nouvelle for lunch at ⑥ **Amal** (see p.149), a culinary training centre for disadvantaged women and a restaurant, serving hearty home-made Moroccan food.

Itinerary

EAT & DRINK

The Moroccan table is the best reflection of the country's rich and multicultural history. Rooted in traditional Berber cuisine, Moroccan food is a fusion of Berber, Arabic and Mediterranean flavours, subtle spices and vibrant colours. Moroccans rarely eat outside of their own homes and as a result, good Moroccan restaurants in Marrakesh can be hard to find. Although, there are a handful of local establishments Marrakeshis flock to when home-cooking isn't an option.

A bustling city by day, Marrakesh turns up the energy after dark. Behind unmarked doors, on lively rooftops and in coveted restaurants, there are enticing pockets of nightlife to be found across the city. The Hivernage has long been synonymous with nightlife in Marrakesh, an area dense with glitzy clubs, sleek hotel bars and much-loved dining institutions, its streets stay abuzz with party-goers until the early hours of the morning. Guéliz/Ville Nouvelle is another part of town flushed with trendy restaurants and bars that lean more local. Beyond the Ville Nouvelle, the historic streets and riads-turned-restaurants of the medina offer a more authentic experience.

Nomad

One of Marrakesh's most coveted restaurants,
boasting unparalleled views.

A multi-tiered restaurant in a prime position between Place des Epices (Spice Market, see p.75) and the souks (see p.73), Nomad brings modern Moroccan dining to the heart of the medina. It was opened in 2014 in an old carpet shop by Kamal Laftimi and Sebastian de Gzell, both well-known Moroccan entrepreneurs, who have a myriad of other successful venues between them (amongst them, Terrasse des Epices, Café des Epices, Le Jardin, Le Kilim and Chichaoua). In many ways, Nomad has been a victim of its own success: the masses have left the space a little tired and a steady flow of first-timers means the menu rarely changes, however it remains the best restaurant in the city for rooftop dining. With panoramic views of the medina and snow-capped Atlas Mountains in the distance, there is no better place to sit on a blue-skied day or clear, starry night.

The modern Moroccan menu leans lighter than its more traditional counterparts and is a welcome relief on hot days or after a stint of heavy eating. A collection of contemporary takes on traditional plates, crowd-pleasers include: crispy courgette (zucchini) fritters, braised lamb shank, roasted cauliflower dowsed in harissa and turmeric butter, and homemade amlou ice-cream (a traditional Moroccan paste of almond, argan oil and honey in ice-cream form). Reservations are essential for a rooftop seat. It's not worth going if you can't sit on the roof.

1 Derb Aarjane

Mon–Sun 12pm–11pm

MAD

80–130 MAD

W

nomadmarrakech.com

Eat & Drink

La Salama

*Traditional Moroccan dining in a modern
setting in the heart of the medina.*

Set across three floors in a building off the chaotic Jemaa el-Fnaa (see p.71), as you ascend the staircase at La Salama, the sounds of the medina fall away and the setting turns into a plush and eccentric dining room of clashing prints and bold colours. The theme continues through to the top floor, a room flooded by natural light, with greenery cascading from the ceiling. The floor-to-ceiling windows offer panoramic views of the orange and red palette of the medina, set against the snow-capped Atlas Mountains in the distance.

A traditional Moroccan menu of tajines, couscous, grilled meats, briwat (puff pastry filled with a range of savoury fillings) and pastilla awaits. The second venue from Moroccan entrepreneur, Nordine Fakir (also behind La Palace, a nightlife destination in Guéliz/Ville Nouvelle), it's no surprise that the atmosphere at La Salama gets lively after dark, bolstered by nightly belly dancing performances, a flowing drinks menu (it is one of very few locations in the medina with a liquor licence) and shisha. Walk-ins for lunch are welcome (tables by the window on the top floor are the best seats in the house during the day). Reservations for dinner are recommended – check their social media channels.

Q		**MAD**
40 Rue des Banques	Mon–Sun 11am–1am	60–190 MAD

Eat & Drink

Le Trou Au Mur

A well-guarded secret by those in-the-know, offering elevated home-style dishes.

---

39 Derb el Farnatchi

Mon & Wed–Sun
12.30pm–3pm &
6.30–11.30pm

MAD
70–190 MAD

W
letrouaumur.com

Tucked away in a labyrinth of winding streets, this restaurant is literally a hidden gem. It is almost impossible to find, so a team of friendly waiters escort diners from the closest main road. Beyond the non-descript door, at the top of a narrow staircase, is a quirky dining room decked-out with pops of lime green and traditional Moroccan paintings. One floor up, a pared-back rooftop offers alfresco dining in the warmer months.

The menu is traditional home-cooking, with elevated family dishes that you won't find outside Moroccan homes. To start, there's tripe, slow-cooked white beans paired with a spicy tomato sauce – typically made to celebrate a child's first tooth – and cherchma, a melange of mixed beans and lentils in a spiced sauce with couscous. For mains, the shoulder mechoui (slow-roasted lamb) is the must-order. To top it off: impeccable service and an exceptional cocktail list – the chilli passionfruit martini is a must. Reservations are essential.

Le Jardin

A leafy restaurant in the heart of the medina.

---

32 Souk Jeld Sidi Abdelaziz

Mon–Sun 10am–11pm

MAD

100 MAD

W

lejardinmarrakech.com

On a narrow street across from Musée de la Femme (see p.81), behind an unassuming door, Le Jardin – true to its name – has a leafy garden, complete with its resident tortoise often found nibbling lettuce at the entrance. Housed in a converted riad (traditional house), with a green tiled courtyard, Le Jardin is constantly abuzz with a lively crowd lunching beneath towering banana trees and wide-brimmed umbrellas.

Opened in 2010, Le Jardin has seen its heyday amongst Marrakeshis, as the menu hasn't changed in recent memory, but it remains a solid spot for lunch for travellers. The menu of traditional Moroccan dishes has hints of European influence, with highlights including: roasted carrot and pistachio salad, a saucy kofta sandwich served with fries and slow-cooked lamb shoulder tajine. Best for lunch, or stop in for an afternoon mint tea or fresh juice. Reservations are recommended, although walk-ins are usually easily accommodated.

Eat & Drink

Shtatto

Marrakesh's newest rooftop eatery-cum-boutique.

---

81 Derb Nkhal Rahba Lakdima

Mon–Sun 9am–11pm

MAD

80 MAD

Located in a prime spot just behind Place des Espices (Spice Market, see p.75), Shtatto is the first concept of its kind in the city: it brings together established and emerging Moroccan artists and designers under one roof. Across three floors, a variety of boutiques showcase some of Marrakesh's best talent in fashion and design (like coveted Moroccan designer, Amine Bendriouich, see p.116 and impeccable leather goods at Nasire, see p.109).

On the third floor, the rooftop presents sweeping views of the medina and beyond, and is lined with comfortable lounge seating, ideal for lingering over lunch or resting weary feet with a fresh juice. A compact open kitchen serves a small menu of seasonal salads and sandwiches, and hearty, filling Moroccan tajines that outshine the rest of the menu. It is a great spot for a casual lunch or a mint tea. There are few better places in the medina to watch the sunset.

Dar Yacout

The darling of
medina dining.

79 Derb Sidi Ahmed Soussi

Tues–Sun 7.30pm–12am

MAD
Set menu, 700 MAD incl. wine

W
daryacout.com

Down a quiet alley in the medina, set in a riad designed by the godfather of contemporary Moroccan interiors, Bill Wills, Dar Yacout's imposing arches, flamboyant motifs and elaborate fireplaces (Wills' trademark design) make a striking backdrop for dinner. Opened in 1990, Dar Yacout was one of the first restaurants of its kind in the medina. Its grandeur has somewhat faded over time but it remains one of the best spots for an over-the-top night out.

A perfected formula, the night starts with an aperitif and panoramic medina views on the rooftop terrace. Next, dinner is an extravagant affair. There is only one option: a set menu of seemingly endless traditional Moroccan dishes in beyond-generous proportions. The experience is bolstered by atmospheric lighting, sumptuous decor and traditional live music nightly. Dar Yacout is best in the warmer months when the internal courtyard is open and tables are set around the lantern-lit pool, under fragrant flowers cascading from neighbouring walls. Reservations are required; for the best seats ask for a poolside table.

Eat & Drink

La Famille

*A welcoming, chic vegetarian
restaurant and boutique.*

On a long and lively street connecting the kasbah (the most ancient part of the medina) to Jemaa el-Fnaa (see p.71), La Famille is a pocket of tranquillity amidst the chaos of the medina. Set outside in a leafy garden, the restaurant offers respite from the crowds and the noise of its surrounds. In stark contrast to the red and orange hues of the streets, La Famille is decked out with a rustic white interior reminiscent of a seaside Mediterranean cafe. Opened by Parisian jewellery designer Stéphanie Giribone, it is run by an all-woman team who exude the warm hospitality that is synonymous with Morocco. A fusion of Moroccan and Mediterranean flavours, for lunch there are three options, changing daily: a hearty salad, pizzetta or simple pasta, all vegetarian and some vegan-friendly.

Open in the afternoon only, the garden packs out with expats and the jet-set crowd looking for a chic and light place to lunch. La Famille is also a good option for a tea or fresh juice for those wanting to rest weary feet after wandering the souk (although, during the lunch-rush tables will often be held for those ordering food). Reservations are recommended – see its social media. Alongside the restaurant, La Famille has a small boutique stocking a selection of jewellery by Stéphanie and a collection of ceramics made in Morocco.

---

34 Derb Jdid	Mon–Sat 12pm–4.30pm	MAD 100 MAD

Eat & Drink

Naranj

*The city's go-to for Lebanese food
in the heart of the medina.*

Opened by Syrian–Lebanese husband-and-wife team, Ruba and Wahib, Naranj is abuzz with an in-the-know crowd looking for an alternative to Moroccan and French cuisine. Naranj was born out of a desire to bring a bit of their native Levant to the bustling streets of the medina. On one of the main veins of the medina connecting Jemaa el-Fnaa (see p.71) to the kasbah (the most ancient part of the medina), nestled in-between street vendors, the restaurant's unassuming facade opens up to a generous space spanning several floors.

There is no better place in the restaurant to sit than on the rooftop terrace – a shady slice of the medina. The black and white tiled tables here are topped with fluffy falafels, crunchy fattoush salad and roasted aubergine (eggplant), alongside heavier plates like fattet batenjain (fried aubergine topped with creamy yoghurt and crunchy croutons) and shawarma (slow-cooked meat, finely sliced and packed into a chewy bread wrap, finished with a tahini sauce). Reservations are recommended, although walk-ins are accommodated when possible.

84 rue Riad Zitoun

Mon–Sat
11.30am–10.30pm

MAD
60–150 MAD

W
naranj.ma

Eat & Drink

El Fenn Bar

*A charismatic bar on the
rooftop of Marrakesh's
most coveted hotel.*

2 Derb Moulay Abdullah
Ben Hezzian

Mon–Sun 5pm–12am

MAD
150 MAD

W
el-fenn.com

Just minutes from Jemaa el-Fnaa (see p.71),
there is no better place to soak in
Marrakesh's skyline than at boutique hotel
El Fenn's rooftop bar. It embodies the
much-loved characteristics of the hotel
(see p.155), opened by Vanessa Branson
and Howell James in 2002 and revamped
with the discerning eye of interior designer
Willem Smit.

The chaos of the city falls away
from this rooftop bar, with sweeping views
of the medina and the Koutoubia Mosque's
famous minaret (see p.87). A solid list of
classic cocktails accompanies a selective list
of French and Moroccan wines. Drinks are
fashionably priced but no more so than other
hotel bars in the city. The perfect place for a
pre-dinner drink, the bar is best in the early
evening before sunset. Take a seat at the oak
bar or at one of the rooftop's many nooks to
watch Marrakesh's skyline turn to a pastel
haze at dusk.

Kabana

The tropics meet Marrakesh's skyline at this buzzing rooftop bar.

---

1 Rue Lalla Fatima Zahra

Mon–Sun 11am–2am

MAD
150 MAD

W
kabana-marrakech.com

The newest bar in Marrakesh is picturesque and sky-lit, in an unmarked building on a bustling street in the heart of the medina, just near Jemaa el-Fnna (see p.71). Kabana's wraparound staircase, lined with black and white photographs of famed actors, opens up to reveal a buzzing rooftop plucked right from a tropical beachside town. The iconic Koutoubia Mosque minaret (see p.87) is so close you feel you could touch it.

Under a string of glowing lanterns, the bar packs out with a mixed crowd who come for sundowners against Marrakesh's pastel skyline and linger longer for the vibe. Some dabble in the fusion menu of tapas, sushi and larger Mediterranean plates but it's best to skip the food and opt for the cocktails. A creative list inspired by travel, each cocktail has a story: ask the waiters to fill you in on the tale behind 'the clutch from little Italy'. Reservations for a seat outside are essential, otherwise walk-ins are welcome.

Al Fassia

Long a local favourite for elevated home-cooking.

Opened in 1987 by husband-and-wife Mohammed and Fatima Chab, Al Fassia has been the city's go-to restaurant for traditional Moroccan cuisine for over three decades. Al Fassia, meaning 'women of Fez' in Arabic, is a tribute to the women and cuisine of the North Moroccan city. Since its beginning, Al Fassia has focused on empowering women through its business, employing an all-woman team. The restaurant is now run by the Chab siblings who expanded the family business, opening a boutique hotel and a second restaurant by the same name on the edge of the Aguedal botanical gardens, a 15-minute drive from the medina.

Al Fassia's original restaurant in Guéliz/Ville Nouvelle is a Marrakesh institution. The interior is a little tired, however it remains a beloved destination for traditional Moroccan cuisine. Its newer sister restaurant, in the garden of the family's hotel, offers alfresco dining on a sprawling terrace. The closest thing to home-cooking available outside of Moroccan homes, both restaurants serve a similar menu of Moroccan classics: flavoursome tajines, fluffy couscous and pastillas (including a solid range of vegetarian options). The order to note: the succulent lamb shoulder, which must be ordered 24 hours in advance. Reservations are essential.

55 Boulevard Zerktouni

Mon–Sun 12pm–2.30pm
& 7.30–11pm

MAD
30–120 MAD

W
al-fassia.com

Eat & Drink

Plus 61

*From Australia to Marrakesh, this buzzing restaurant
brings a fresh approach to the city's dining scene.*

A Marrakesh hotspot nestled amongst a pocket of trendy boutiques,
museums and contemporary galleries in Guéliz/Ville Nouvelle, Plus 61's
simple Australian-inspired menu and its bright minimalistic interior are a
blissful break from the sensory overload of the Red City. Opened in 2019
by Australian expat Cassandra Karinsky, after living in Marrakesh for over a
decade, the restaurant has been welcomed with open arms by locals looking
for something beyond traditional Moroccan and French, the two cuisines that
dominate Marrakesh's restaurant scene.

The dishes are inspired by the diversity of Australian cuisine and
draw on Asian, Mediterranean and Middle Eastern flavours for a fresh and
simple menu. Australian chef Andrew Cibej pairs local seasonal ingredients
with house-made staples (all of the bread, pasta and dairy products are made
in-house) to create relaxed dishes with elements that subtly nod to Moroccan
cuisine. The menu changes regularly based on the availability of produce
but highlights have included: crunchy grissini with amlou (a traditional
Moroccan paste of argan oil, almond and honey), mussel ragu and crispy
falafel served with tahini yogurt. To complement the food is a tightly curated
selection of French and Moroccan wine, solid cocktails and fresh juices.
Plus 61 packs out daily with its regular crowd who come to enjoy its unique
offerings and impeccable service, so reservations are recommended.

MAD

96 Rue Mohammed   Mon–Sat   30–120 MAD
   el Beqal   12pm–10pm

W

plus61.com

Eat & Drink

Amal

*A community training centre for women and
a restaurant with philanthropy at its core.*

Founded by American–Moroccan Nora Fitzgerald Belahcen, Amal, meaning hope in Arabic, is a non-profit organisation set in a converted house in Guéliz/Ville Nouvelle that trains disadvantaged women in its culinary training centre. It offers women the opportunity to learn cooking skills and gain hands-on experience in the restaurant. Surrounded by a garden that serves as outdoor dining, a team of Amal's smiling trainees in bright orange aprons busily move around serving food and attending to tables.

The restaurant is open for breakfast and lunch daily. A traditional Moroccan breakfast of Hssoua Belboula (a creamy soup made with barley and milk) is served, and for lunch two daily options are written up on a chalkboard. Amal has struck a chord with the local community, who come in droves to support it and enjoy the familial cooking. It is abuzz on Friday when the restaurant fills up with locals who come for a lunch of couscous following afternoon prayer (a weekly tradition in Morocco). Reservations are recommended. Amal also offers traditional Moroccan cooking classes by appointment at its second training centre in Targa (about 12 minutes' drive from the restaurant). Check its website for information and to book.

  MAD

Cnr Rue Allal Ben Ahmed   Mon–Sun 8.30–10.30am   30 MAD
& Rue Ibn Sina   & 12pm–3.30pm

 **W**

amalnonprofit.org

Eat & Drink

Grand Café de la Poste

A French brasserie with a rich history in the heart of Guéliz/Ville Nouvelle.

Cnr Blvd El Mansour Eddahbi & Rue el Imam Malik

Mon–Sun 8am–1am

MAD
150–250 MAD

W
grandcafedelaposte.restaurant

Set in a 1920s building that once housed the French colonial post office and adjoining cafe during the French Protectorate (1912–56), Grand Café de la Poste embodies the spirit and glamour of the roaring twenties. Overlooking Place du Novembre 16, a busy intersection, its street-side terrace is a popular daytime spot, abuzz with a mixed crowd of foreigners and well-heeled Moroccans socalising over coffee and mint tea.

Beyond the humble facade, a sense of nostalgia engulfs a moody dining room that hosts diners enjoying a menu of French classics like duck confit and beef tartare, accompanied by French and Moroccan wines. Wicker tables on the semi-exterior terrace, protected from the street by billowing drapes, offer a more relaxed setting that packs out for lunch and after dinner, with those in-the-know stopping by for a nightcap. Desserts like chocolate fondant and tarte aux pommes (apple pie) are so good they almost outshine the rest of the menu. Reservations are recommended.

Baromètre

No other bar in Marrakesh takes its mixology as seriously.

Rue Moulay Ali

Mon–Sat 6.30pm–1.30am

MAD

150 MAD

Marked by an oversized B sitting on the sidewalk in Guéliz/Ville Nouvelle, Baromètre is akin to the low-lit speakeasies found behind unmarked doors in New York and London. Opened by the Hadni brothers, part of a new generation of Moroccan entrepreneurs contemporising the Red City, the service is anything but snooty, with a team of welcoming staff and energetic bartenders.

Housed in a basement with no windows, the pared-back interior leaves the bar to do the talking. While Marrakesh isn't known for its cutting-edge cocktail culture, the drinks here are complex and creative. A robust line-up of reinvented classics and unique cocktails are served with panache in bespoke glassware best suited to the drink. A good spot for a pre- or post-dinner drink (the later it is, the livelier the venue tends to be), take a seat at the bar to be close to the action.

Eat & Drink

Comptoir Darna

This beloved restaurant is a mainstay
of Marrakesh nightlife.

The go-to dinner with a show in Marrakesh, Comptoir Darna is all about theatrics. Affectionately referred to as 'Le Comptoir' by Marrakeshis, this restaurant-cum-club opened in 1999 and is a fixture in Marrakesh's nightlife scene. Amid a cluster of restaurants and clubs in the party-centric Hivernage, a mixed crowd of tourists and locals packs out the plush, red dining room night after night. By no means the best culinary experience in town, Comptoir Darna's reputation lies in the spectacle of entertainment that it rolls out nightly.

A traditional orchestra lined along the imposing staircase opens each night with classical Moroccan music. But the real action starts at 10pm when glamourous belly dancers twirl around the restaurant in a choreographed blur. A hit-and-miss mix of traditional Moroccan and international cuisine, the entertainment mostly outshines the food. As the night goes on, diners pack out the back garden for post-dinner shisha and cocktails. On the weekends, as night inches closer to early morning, the whole place turns more club than restaurant, as the DJ settles in and the area nearby the upstairs bar turns into a dance floor. Admittedly, the whole shebang is a tad cheesy but it's a must-have Marrakesh experience for first-timers. Reservations are required, opt for a table on the second floor for a more intimate experience.

Avenue Echouhada,
Hivernage

Mon–Sun 7.30pm–3am
(kitchen closes 1am)

MAD
150 MAD +

W
comptoirmarrakech.com

Eat & Drink

Bô Zin

*North Africa meets Asia at Marrakesh's
hottest nightlife destination.*

A sought-after venue since it opened its door in 2018, this is where well-heeled Moroccans and the jet-set crowd come to play and be seen. From the French hospitality group also behind Grand Café de la Poste (see p.52), Bô Zin has perfected the nightlife formula: flowing booze and an Asian fusion menu and mainstream music. A hybrid indoor–outdoor space, the restaurant flows seamlessly between the cosy lounge-like interior and the plush garden. Outside, under billowing drapes, tables are threaded around a flowing bar where a chic crowd hovers, bopping to the tracks of the nightly DJ.

Dinner is on the pricier side by Marrakesh standards and, while it offers a decent selection of dim sum and options like prawn teppanyaki and vegetable couscous for good measure, it's not the drawcard. A more enticing cocktail list and a buzzing vibe attracts party-goers, especially on the weekends when Bô Zin is most alive. Arrive later in the evening and opt for a table outside to be in the thick of the action. A 20-minute drive from the medina, it is best to pre-arrange transport back as taxis lingering out the front of the restaurant will charge a premium for a ride home, especially as the night gets on. A smart-casual dress code is observed. Reservations are required.

MAD

Route de l'Ourika   Mon–Sun 8pm–late   200 MAD +

W

bo-zin.com

STREET
FOOD

One of Marrakesh's best-kept culinary secrets is its street
food. The weaving alleys of the medina are dotted with
vibrant local establishments, serving rich and flavoursome
dishes that out-do the food found in most restaurants. This
is where you will find Marrakeshis eating: at street-side carts,
hole-in-the-wall eateries and low-key cafes enjoying beloved
Moroccan staples and some of the best food in the city.

Eating street food requires a certain sense of adventure, a
willingness to nudge up alongside locals at shared tables, look
past aesthetics and work through language barriers to order.
But it is worth it for mouth-watering, inexpensive food and a
truly local experience. From mechoui (slow-roasted lamb) at
Chez Lamine (see p.61) to flaky m'semen (crepe) at Zahra's
(see p.65), this chapter includes the city's must-try street foods
and the best places to get them. Now to navigate the medina
to find them!

Chez Lamine

A must-have Marrakesh experience
for meat-lovers.

On a small alley flanked on one side by stalls selling fragrant fresh mint, other herbs and olives, and the souks (see p.73), Chez Lamine is a Marrakesh establishment. Found amongst a row of vendors all selling mechoui (slow-roasted lamb cooked in underground clay pits for several hours), tucked off the bustling Jemaa el-Fnaa (see p.71), it is part of what is affectionately referred to as mechoui alley. Bypass the first few stalls and go to the end of the alley, marked by an oversized Chez Lamine sign, where you'll find a flurry of activity as a team of men hoist lambs from the underground pit behind them up onto the street-side counter for carving.

The meat is sold by weight so ask for *nus* (half a kilo) or *rub* (quarter), or judge the amount by eye. You'll then be seated in the makeshift restaurant one stall over and served your selection of lamb, with warm bread and a steaming mint tea. You can be seated in the restaurant and order with the waiters, but it's better to order at the counter, as having the lamb carved in front of you is part of the experience. This part of the medina packs out for lunch each day with Marrakeshis and those in-the-know, so it's best to arrive around 1pm but not too much later, as this popular spot sells out of lamb fast. Along with mechoui, sheep's head – a local delicacy – is also served.

29 Rue Ibn Aïcha	Mon–Sun 12pm–3pm	**MAD** 80 MAD

Street Food

No. 14 (Fried Fish)

Eating amongst the mayhem of this makeshift food market is a must.

Jemaa el-Fnaa

Mon–Sun 7pm–late

MAD

50 MAD

Like clockwork at dusk each day, hundreds of food stands abruptly appear in the middle of Jemaa el-Fnaa (see p.71). Swarming with touts waving menus, this food market serving everything from traditional tajine to snail soup, may appear like a tourist trap but this is where many Marrakeshis eat every evening. Bypass the touts (politely saying you have already eaten does the trick) and follow Moroccans as they confidently weave through the crowds to their favourite stands.

Marked only by a tiny sign, No. 14 is on the southern end of Jemaa el-Fnaa and if have to ask for directions, it's best to ask the vendors that line the square – rather than the questionable touts. Line up with the locals and order the fish of the day, served freshly fried in a light batter with a side of handcut fries.

Chez Abdelouahed (No. 66)

A must-eat street food staple at a stand crowded with locals.

Jemaa el-Fnaa

Mon–Sun 7pm–late

MAD

50 MAD

Crazy sandwich, known as khobz majnona in Arabic and sandwich de fou in French, is one of the city's best-kept culinary secrets, so much so that when you ask for it, especially in Arabic, the locals will affectionately laugh. Khobz majnona is traditional bread stuffed with potatoes and boiled eggs, and topped with a healthy drizzle of olive oil, cumin and harissa, and is sold at countless places across the city. The best place to eat it is at Chez Abdelouahed (No. 66). Part of the makeshift food market that pops up in Jemaa el-Fnaa (see p.71) each evening, this is one of the only stands without a tout trying to draw in tourists.

There is a crowd of locals, several rows deep, huddled around this stand all night, so you'll need to be patient for a seat. Order a khobz majnona and a mint tea, and soak up the experience of eating amongst the mayhem of Jemaa el-Fnaa.

M'semen at Zahra's

Try m'semen, the cornerstone of Moroccan breakfasts, at this popular local spot.

Warm, flakey, fluffy and chewy all at the same time, m'semen is an everyday Moroccan staple. Made from a mixture of flour, semolina, water, sugar and salt, and cooked on a hot plate greased with oil or butter, m'semen is often thought of as Morocco's version of a pancake or crepe. Typically served with honey in the morning and as widespread as mint tea, there is no shortage of places to eat m'semen in Marrakesh. However, for the best m'semen and a truly local experience, find Zahra.

In the heart of El Moukef, a heaving neighbourhood in the east of the medina, Zahra's stand is on a refreshingly open street. In the evening, this part of the city is so packed with locals socialising over mint tea and food from neighbouring stands, it's hard to move around. By morning, the pace slows down and the sound of Arabic chatter, loud music and buzz of motorbikes falls away to the low hum of everyday life. There you'll find Zahra, serving her m'semen from a makeshift stand, set against a pastel orange wall. Take a seat alongside her regular crowd, order a m'semen with honey and a mint tea, and watch daily life in the medina go by. It can be difficult to find Zahra as her stand has no official address. Use a map to search 'Place Moukef' and this should you lead you to the correct area, then use street names to navigate to her.

		MAD
The start of Rue Bin Lafnadek (close to cnr Ave Bab El Khemis)	Mon–Sun 8–11.30am	10 MAD

Street Food

Sfenj

A Moroccan staple, sweet or savoury sfenj is best from this locally-loved stand.

---

3 Rue Bab Agnaou, Kasbah

Mon–Thurs &
Sat–Sun 8–11.30am

MAD
1 MAD

Sfenj is the Maghreb's doughnut: airy, spongy rings of dough deep-fried in oil and sprinkled with sugar or eaten with honey. Sfenj is typically eaten in the morning or as an afternoon snack and can be either served sweet or savoury without any toppings. In the south of the medina just minutes from Bab Agnaou, the striking gate that functions as the entrance to the ancient royal area of the kasbah, this stand is known for having some of the best sfenj in Marrakesh.

Not easily found via maps, to find this stand, make your way to Bab Agnaou, keep the gate to your left and take the first left, and you'll see this stand on the right after a few metres. Join the steady stream of locals each morning for sfenj and mint tea before exploring the Saadian Tombs (see p.89), just metres away, and the stunning architecture of Bahia Palace (see p.93), a short walk to the east.

Harrira at Fadma's

*A treasured local spot
serving traditional
Moroccan soup.*

cnr Ave Hommane Al
Fatouaki & Rue El Moustachfa
(opposite Académie de
l'Education Nationale)

Mon–Sun from 5pm
until soup runs out

MAD

5 MAD

Ask Marrakeshis in the medina where they
eat harrira and Fadma's name is echoed
time and time again. Just minutes from
Jemaa el-Fnaa (see p.71), you'll find her
serving harrira soup to her regulars each
evening from a makeshift set-up tucked
behind a beautiful horseshoe-shaped arch.
A traditional Moroccan tomato-based soup
with chickpea, lentils and a blend of herbs
and mild spices, the harrira here is served
piping hot from an oversized pot perched
up on the main table. From around 5pm each
day, this place is bustling with Marrakeshis
crouched over the long trestle tables slurping
up hearty harrira from long wooden spoons.
Typically eaten during Ramadan in
Morocco to break fast, the soup is also an
everyday staple eaten as an early evening
snack or as an entrée.

EXPLORE

Marrakesh is steeped in rich history and offers a wealth of museums, monuments, gardens and galleries to explore. From the Almoravid dynasty, that founded the city in 1062, to the Alaouites and the empires that reigned in between, each of the country's rulers built mosques, palaces, elaborate gardens and lavish burial sites. Many of these sites have been restored and opened to the public, offering a fascinating insight into Marrakesh's past. The city also boasts a diverse cultural and art scene. From the wave of 19th-century Orientalist artists to Yves Saint Laurent in the 1960s, Marrakesh's exotica has long attracted creative souls looking for inspiration.

Across the city, riads (traditional Moroccan houses characterised by an interior courtyard) and old buildings have been transformed into galleries, and a burgeoning contemporary art scene has made Marrakesh the international destination for contemporary African art. Whether it be strolling through the city's famed souks (see p. 73) or historic square Jemaa el-Fnaa (see p. 71), admiring the decorative design of Bahia Palace (see p. 93) and exotic flora of Jardin Majorelle (see p. 97) or browsing the contemporary African art at MACAAL (see p. 105), Marrakesh is a rousing city to explore.

Jemaa el-Fnaa

*This fascinating square has been
the pulsating centre of the city for centuries.*

Part of the UNESCO World Heritage site known for its cultural significance, and both a major tourist attraction and a part of everyday life for Moroccans living in the medina, Jemaa el-Fnaa has served as a meeting point and marketplace for thousands of years. By day the square is occupied by a handful of snake charmers and fresh orange juice carts. But like clockwork just before sunset each day, the food stands, henna artists, fortune tellers, street performers, musicians, acrobats, comedians and snake charmers emerge to start their day's work and by nightfall the square has erupted into a chaotic carnival. Historically the main stage for hakawatis (master storytellers), who would draw crowds of hundreds here nightly, unfortunately nowadays the storytellers are few and far between.

Jemaa el-Fnaa is the city's best form of entertainment but it is also notorious for pickpockets and swindlers. Be on guard against them and the henna artists too, who are known to grab and decorate the hands of unsuspecting tourists, forcing them into payment. If you watch a performer or take photos, giving small change is expected. If you are approached for more money, don't be intimidated into over paying.

Each night the high cafe terraces that line the square pack out with tourists and locals sipping mint tea and enjoying the nightly spectacle from above. Café de France in the southern corner of the square is an institution and offers uninterrupted bird's-eye views from its upper terraces. Arrive early to nab the best seats.

| Jemaa el-Fnaa | Daily 24-hours | jemaa-el-fna.com |

Explore

Souk

The beating heart of the medina is an enchanting marketplace, full of life and unique items.

The souk is a lively labyrinth of marketplaces and a dizzying honeycomb of alleyways. Getting lost is inevitable and part of the experience. The least confusing entry point is found on the northern end of Jemaa el-Fnaa (see p. 71), where a line of stalls frame dimly lit alleys that lead into the souk. Merchants riding donkeys from afar have been replaced by buzzing motorbikes zipping through the narrow alleys, so watch your step.

The souk may appear to be a chaotic collection of artisans and merchants but each section is organised by a particular product or trade: Souk Sammarine (textiles and souvenirs); Souk Smata (colourful babouches: Moroccan slippers); Souk Cherratine (leather goods, like bags and belts); Souk Haddadine (metalwork); Souk des Bijoutiers (traditional jewellery) and Souk de Teinturiers, the fabric dyer's market, is full of alleys draped in brightly coloured materials. Souk Attarine was originally dedicated to spices and perfumes, and today also sells clusters of glowing lanterns, lamps, mirrors and silverwear.

While some products are unique to specific vendors, many import the same products from around Morocco and beyond. Be prepared to spend time haggling (see p.170) but remember to start with pleasantries, bargain in good nature and enjoy the theatrics of it all. While more crowded than at other times of the day, the souk is best visited in the afternoon when it is most alive, especially on Fridays when many vendors remain closed until after afternoon prayer. If you intend to do some serious shopping, opt for earlier in the day as less crowds will make it easier to move around.

Medina

Mon–Sun
10am–7pm

Explore

Place des Epices (Spice Market)

The epicentre of the souk, this vibrant square brims with spice stalls and carpet vendors.

Just as the souk (see p.73) begins to seem never-ending, its dim alleyways open up to reveal a colourful square offering a brief respite, although no less chaotic than the souk. Much like Jemaa el-Fnaa (see p.71), Place des Epices (Rahba Lakdima in Arabic) is a continuous theatre and the merchants are the stars of the show. Flanked by spice vendors and dubious herbalists on one side and carpet traders on the other, it's a boisterous scene of colours and scents. Enticing spices are piled in cylinders: cumin, coriander, cinnamon, star anise, saffron and ras el-hanout (an earthy blend used widely in Moroccan cooking). Be vigilant when buying spices as these vendors are as cheeky as they are charming. One of the tricks of the trade is to swap the spices given as a sample for a lesser quality product when bagging up orders.

Across the square, behind the piles of raffia bags and baskets, framed by traditional carpets strung from surrounding buildings and marked only by a small blue and yellow sign, is an endless burrow of carpet traders. On six days a week around 4pm, the burrow erupts into a hive of activity when traders, known as dalaleen, come down from the mountains to sell their rugs. If you are interested in buying a rug, visit the store just after the orange sign on the left-hand side of the alley (directly across from the jewellery shop). You can sit and enjoy fresh mint tea with a member of the Sabîi family, while they explain the weaves, symbols and colours of their carpets. Back outside, watch all the action of the square from the street-side terrace at Café des Epices, or for a bird's-eye view grab a seat on the rooftop at Nomad (see p.33).

Place des Epices

Mon–Sun approx. 10am–7pm

Explore

Medersa Ben Youssef

*A centuries-old Islamic school, with a tranquil
courtyard and breathtaking architecture.*

Founded in the mid-14th century, Medersa Ben Youssef was once the largest
Islamic school in North Africa. The medersa (school in Arabic) takes its
name from neighbouring Ali Ben Youssef mosque, to which it was formerly
attached. Once home to 900 students, the school was an important centre
of learning and religion for more than four centuries. The first iteration of the
school built by Sultan Abou el Hassan in the mid-14th century was modest
compared with the structure that stands today. The lavish redesign can be
attributed to Abdallah al-Ghalibwho, the Saadian Sultan who reconstructed
and expanded it in 1564. From the outside the medersa blends into its
surrounds, with only an Arabic calligraphic inscription that translates to:
'you who enter my door, may your highest hopes be exceeded', hinting at
what is behind its walls.

Inside, an exquisite central courtyard highlights the intricate Islamic
architecture. Around the courtyard, blue and green zellige (mosaic tiles)
stop halfway up the wall to meet dusty orange stucco inscribed with Islamic
invocations, which then effortlessly gives way to intricate cedar woodwork.
Overlooking the courtyard are the tiny windows of the student dormitories,
a network of some 130 crammed rooms. Off the courtyard is a beautiful
prayer room characterised by three arches supported by marble columns
and an engraved cedar dome ceiling. Check before visiting as the school was
closed at time of writing for an extensive restoration that is expected to be
completed towards the end of 2020.

MAD

Place Ben Youssef   Mon–Sun 9am–5pm   60 MAD

Explore

Maison de la Photographie

*A photography museum with a unique collection
of historic Moroccan photographs.*

Opened in 2009, Maison de la Photographie is a private photography museum described by its founders, Hamid Mergani and Patrick Manac'h, as an archive of Morocco. Housed in a converted riad, the museum's crisp white walls, a stark contrast to the orange and red hues of the medina just outside, tell stories of Moroccan life between the 1870s and 1950s. The exhibition of exclusively black and white photographs from Mergani and Manac'h's private collection, documents social and cultural developments in Morocco throughout the decades. The collection also highlights technical advances in photography, as seen in the style and quality of the images across certain periods in history, and includes the first photograph ever taken in the country in 1862. It also includes the oldest collection of glass negatives taken of the Atlas Mountains.

Wrapping around the open-air courtyard, the museum's three floors are organised by region and theme. Across each section the photographs depict various historical and cultural aspects of life in Morocco. Berbers, Morocco's Indigenous population, feature prominently in the exhibition. The museum also has a small cinema on its upper floor (showing Daniel Chicault's *Landscapes and Faces of the High Atlas*, a documentary about Berber tribes of the High Atlas) and a small cafe on its rooftop. One of the highest in the area, the rooftop boasts uninterrupted views of the medina and beyond.

---

46 Rue Souk Ahal Fassi

Mon–Sun 9.30am–7pm

MAD

50 MAD entry

W

maisondelaphotographie.ma

Explore

Musée de la Femme

The first museum of its kind in North Africa, it is dedicated to the history and culture of Moroccan women.

Opened in September 2018 by Nizar Gartit, Musée de la Femme is a unique addition to Marrakesh's growing cultural scene, which pays homage to the women of Morocco. Located next to Medersa Ben Youssef (See p.77), the multi-tiered space hosts multimedia exhibitions that highlight the role of Moroccan women in the country's social and political landscape. Ranging from prominent women, who are known as pioneers in their respective fields, to the unknown women of small villages, the exhibitions aim to celebrate all kinds of Moroccan women across photography and mixed media works. The museum also provides a space on its second floor for emerging contemporary female artists to showcase their work.

    The exhibitions are curated by founder Nizar Gartit, who also oversees the exhibitions at Maison de la Photographie (See p.79). The museum's first exhibition was dedicated to rural women, highlighting their role in the daily life of the family, the village and the community. The second exhibition focused on the women who laid the foundations of contemporary Morocco, like Touria Chaoui: Morocco's first female pilot, Izza Genini: the first Moroccan woman to make a documentary and Laïla Alaoui: a prominent Moroccan photographer. Exhibitions change every six months or so, see the museum's website for details.

---

19 Rue Sidi Abdel Aziz

Mon–Sun
9.30am–6.30pm

MAD

30 MAD

W

museedelafemme.ma

Explore

The Orientalist Museum

Morocco is shown through the lens of foreign artists who lived or travelled in the country.

A private and intimate museum, the eponymous Orientalist Museum is dedicated to Orientalism. Flanked by Maison de la Photographie (see p.79) and Medersa Ben Youssef (see p.77), the museum exhibits a private collection of paintings that portray Morocco through the eyes of foreign artists. Often criticised as having a colonial and political agenda, Orientalist art can also be a genuine attempt by the artist to recreate their experiences. The Orientalist Museum sparks this dialogue in the context of a collection of paintings that provide a fascinating insight into the artists' perceptions of the Maghreb and beyond.

Set in a beautifully restored 17th-century riad (a traditional Moroccan house characterised by an internal courtyard), the space boasts beautiful Moorish features, such as zellige (mosaic tiles) on its floors, intricate woodwork, large pillars decorated with carvings and the towering arches of the central courtyard. Hung on the walls are the works of famous Orientalist artists, such as Eugène Delacroix, Matteo Brondy and Jacques Majorelle (his Cubist villa studio can be seen at Jardin Majorelle, see p.97), alongside sporadic pieces of traditional furniture, jewellery and ceramics.

Place des Epices   Mon–Sun 10am–7pm   **MAD**
50 MAD

W
theorientalistmuseumofmarrakech.
business.site

Explore

Marrakesh Museum

*Housed in a 19th-century palace, the museum is a
stunning example of Moorish architecture.*

Adjacent to Medersa Ben Youssef (see p.77), this museum started its life
as Dar Menebhi, the palace of Medi Menebhi, Morocco's defence minister
during the reign of Alaouite Sultan Moulay Abdelaziz. After Morocco's
independence from the French Protectorate in 1956, the palace was seized by
the state and went on to become home to Morocco's first school for girls in
1967. Several decades later, the palace was bought by the Omar Benjelloun
Foundation and, following an extensive restoration, it opened its doors as a
museum in 1997. Many of the former palace's features have been preserved,
and today the building functions as both a museum and a reference for
Moorish architecture and design.

    The internal courtyard forms the heart of the museum, with the
rooms around it housing the collection of Moroccan artefacts. Originally an
open-air courtyard, the room has been enclosed by a glass ceiling and houses
a striking chandelier hung above three marble basins. While modifications
to the palace have been made, many of its original Moorish features remain:
zellige (mosaic tiles), horseshoe archways and high ceilings adorned with
muqarnas (intricate 3D carvings in geometric designs). The museum's
exhibition is formed by a haphazard, yet interesting collection of Moroccan
artefacts: ceramics, traditional jewellery and clothing, ancient coins and
Orientalist paintings.

Place Ben Youssef

Mon–Sun 9am–6.30pm

MAD
30 MAD

Explore

Le Jardin Secret

A unique garden hidden behind towering walls.

Le Jardin Secret (secret garden) is a plush sanctuary with a rich history in the heart of the medina. It started its life as a palace built by a Saadian sultan in the late 16th century. Two centuries later it became the opulent home of a prominent Islamic figure in Marrakesh and remained so until 1934. It was restored and opened to the public in 2016.

121 Rue Mouassine

Mon–Sun 9.30am–6pm

MAD

60 MAD garden entry, an extra 35 MAD for tower access

W

lejardinsecretmarrakech.com

The property's towering walls envelop two distinct gardens: an exotic garden planted with plants and trees from all over the world, and an Islamic garden that is the larger of the two. The Islamic garden is divided into four parts by water channels, pathways and shaded pavilions, reflecting the four gardens of paradise described in the Qur'an. The Islamic garden is flanked by exhibition spaces, offering a wealth of information about the history and architecture of the property. Overlooking the garden is an imposing tower that offers a bird's-eye perspective of its unique design, as well as medina views.

Koutoubia Mosque

An enduring symbol of the Red City.

Jemaa el-Fnaa

Mon–Sun 9am–6pm

mosquee-koutoubia.com

Built in the 12th century by the Almohad dynasty, the Koutoubia Mosque is the city's most prominent landmark. The highest point in Marrakesh at 77 metres (252 feet) tall, its minaret, topped with three golden brass balls and beautifully decorated with various motifs, towers over Jemaa el-Fnaa (see p.71). One of two mosques built on the site, the first was built in 1147 and, though the exact dates are unknown, construction of the present-day mosque is thought to have begun that same year to correct a misalignment with Mecca in the first. The two mosques stood side-by-side for several decades, however only the second mosque stands today.

As with all Moroccan mosques, the Koutoubia Mosque is reserved for Muslims only. Behind the mosque, in the shadow of its minaret, are the Koutoubia's gardens: a lush green space accessible to everyone and filled with fragrant orange trees, wide walkways and water fountains.

Explore

Saadian Tombs

With little trace of their rule left in Marrakesh,
the tombs are a key site of the Saadian dynasty.

Hidden for over two centuries, the Saadian tombs are an opulent burial site of the Saadian dynasty that ruled Morocco from 1549 to 1659. The origins of the burial site pre-date his time but it was Ahmed al-Mansur, the Saadian sultan who ruled from 1578 to 1603, who undertook the expansion and embellishment of the necropolis. Upon entering through a discreet entrance in the heart of the kasbah (the most ancient part of the medina), the dusty street morphs into the opulent complex that al-Mansur envisaged for the afterlife. A flowering garden, that houses the more humble graves of important Saadian figures, is framed by the intricate mausoleums al-Mansur built for his family. For his own mausoleum, the Chamber of 12 Pillars, al-Mansur spared no expense. A breathtaking display of Moroccan craftsmanship, the room is decorated with a mosaic floor, towering pillars built from imported Italian Carrara and a finely crafted cedar ceiling.

    After the fall of the Saadian dynasty, Ismail ibn Sharif, the second ruler of the Alaouite dynasty, ordered the destruction of all Saadian monuments. Fearful of destroying the burial ground, he superstitiously spared the Saadian tombs and instead sealed the complex from the public view. Immured for almost two centuries, the tombs were discovered by chance in 1917 during an aerial survey of the area and soon after were restored and opened once again. Near the exit, a small outdoor theatre runs a documentary about the tombs in a range of languages and it's worth sticking around to watch it.

Rue de La Kasbah

Mon–Sun 9am–5pm

MAD

70 MAD

W

tombeaux-saddiens.com

Explore

El Badi Palace

The foundations of a once opulent palace guarded
by storks who nest on its towering walls.

Built to commemorate Morocco's victory over Portugal in the 1578 Battle of Three Kings, today only the ruins of El Badi Palace remain. In the wake of their victory, the then sultan, Abu Marwan Abd al-Malik demanded a large financial payout from the Portuguese. Al-Malik's brother and successor, Ahmed al-Mansur used the money to build El Badi Palace, sparing no expense to create a symbol of victory and power. Its construction took place between 1578 and 1594 and, on its completion, it was the grandest palace of its time, however its glory was short-lived. When they came into power in 1659, the Alaouites were determined to destroy all traces of the Saadian dynasty so they stripped the palace of its valuables and left it in ruins.

Although only the foundation of the palace remains, the original structure is thought to have had over 360 rooms, an enormous courtyard, pools, lavish reception halls and summer pavilions all adorned with opulent finishes. Wandering around the sprawling grounds, you get a sense of what an extraordinary place it must have been. Today in the south-west and south-east corners of the complex are two gallery spaces offering a wealth of knowledge about the palace and other key sites in Marrakesh. In the south-east corner, the original minbar (pulpit) of the Koutoubia Mosque (see p.87) is displayed. A masterpiece of Islamic art, the wooden minbar was built in 1137 by craftsman in Cordova, Spain and moved to El Badi Palace in 1962 after its restoration.

♀	⊘	**MAD**
Ksibat Nhass	Mon–Sun 9am–5pm	70 MAD

W
palais-el-badi.com

Explore

Bahia Palace

*A vast complex with tranquil courtyards and stunning details
in every room.*

On the outskirts of the Mellah, an area in the south-east of the medina
once home to Marrakesh's Jewish population, Bahia Palace was built in two
stages over several decades towards the end of the 19th century. One of
Marrakesh's most impressive examples of Moroccan craftsmanship, it was
first commissioned by Si Moussa, a former slave who climbed the ranks
to become the grand vizir to Sultan Hussan I. Si Moussa set out to create
an opulent private residence known as Dar Si Moussa (Dar means house).
After his death, his son Ba Ahmed succeeded his father as grand vizir and
continued construction of the palace. After Sultan Hussan I's death, Ba
Ahmed became the de facto ruler of Morocco after enthroning his young
nephew as sultan. With his newfound power, Ba Ahmed expanded the palace,
hiring artisans from all over North Africa to create a luxurious residence that
housed his four wives and several concubines.

By the time of his death in 1900, the palace was an intricate complex
comprising over 150 rooms, each richly decorated from floor-to-ceiling with
traditional zellige (mosaic tiles) and intricate zouak (painted wood) ceilings.
Due to its staged construction, Bahia is a maze-like structure of living areas,
separated by fragrant courtyard gardens in geometric patterns. Today, the
rooms of the palace are empty and only a portion is open to the public. The
private section is used on occasion by the royal family.

Avenue Imam El Ghazali

Mon–Sun 9am–5pm

MAD

70 MAD entry

W

palais-bahia.com

Explore

Yves Saint Laurent Museum

*On his namesake street, this museum is dedicated to the life
and work of the iconic French fashion designer.*

In the modern neighbourhood of Guéliz/Ville Nouvelle, the museum's
sprawling terracotta building blends effortlessly into its earthy surrounds,
with only the shining YSL logo signalling its presence. A project overseen by
Yves Saint Laurent's partner Pierre Bergé, the museum pays homage to the
late fashion designer in a city that played a pivotal role in his career. Saint
Laurent's love affair with Marrakesh began when he first visited with Bergé
in 1966. In the years that followed, Marrakesh became a creative retreat for
Saint Laurent and its influence inspired his work in the form of bold colours.
    The sprawling museum comprises two exhibition halls, a gallery
space, a research library with more than 5000 books about Berber culture,
botany and the history of fashion (accessible by appointment only), a 150-
seat auditorium, bookstore and terrace cafe. The main exhibition space,
a dark room in the heart of the museum, displays a collection of 50 of Saint
Laurent's key pieces, from a collection of over 5000 garments stored in the
museum's basement. Amongst them are four of his most iconic designs:
'le Smoking', the first tuxedo designed for women; the Mondrian dress; the
safari jacket and the pea coat. Outside the permanent collection, the works
of upcoming Moroccan and international designers and artists are shown in a
temporary exhibition space.

Rue Yves Saint Laurent

Mon–Sun 9.30am–6pm
(last admission 5.30pm)

MAD
100 MAD entry

W
museeyslmarrakech.com

Explore

Jardin Majorelle

*This botanical garden's legacy is of great artists
who shared a love for Marrakesh.*

Jardin Majorelle is one of the world's most unique and vibrant gardens. It began its life in the early 1920s when French Orientalist painter, Jacques Majorelle, bought a block of land on the outskirts of the medina. He set about building his home and the exotic two and half acre garden we know today, a project that took him over 40 years to create. In 1931, Majorelle commissioned Paul Sinior to design a Cubist villa to house his workshop and studio. The ground floor of the villa is now home to the Berber Museum (see p.99).

A passionate botanist, Majorelle filled the land around the villa with exotic plants from all around the world. He planted a dense collection of cacti, palm trees, bamboo, agaves, rare trees, vines and ferns along intertwining walkways, approaching the garden's composition like a painting. Around 1937 he started painting the garden's surrounds in bold colours, covering the villa in cobalt blue, now known as Majorelle blue. Due to high maintenance costs, Majorelle opened the garden to the public in 1947 for a small entrance fee. After his death in 1962, the garden remained open but began to fall into disrepair until 1980, when it was bought and restored by Yves Saint Laurent and his partner, Pierre Bergé.

MAD

Rue Yves Saint Laurent | Mon–Sun 8am–5.30pm | 30 MAD entry

W

jardinmajorelle.com

Explore

Berber Museum

*An informative museum devoted to Morocco's
Indigenous population.*

Set in the heart of the Jardin Majorelle (see p.97) and housed in the former studio of French painter Jacques Majorelle, the Berber Museum showcases the history and culture of the Imazighen, also known as Berbers, a group indigenous to Morocco and other parts of North Africa. It is one part of Yves Saint Laurent's legacy in Marrakesh, which includes the Jardin Majorelle and the neighbouring Yves Saint Laurent Museum (see p.95). The museum displays artefacts from the personal collection of the iconic designer and his partner, Pierre Bergé. The pair were captivated by Berber culture and their collection of over six hundred objects portrays the traditions and culture of ancient and nomadic Berber tribes, spanning regions from the High Atlas Mountains to the Sahara Desert.

The atmospherically dark museum, juxtaposed by the lush and electric colouring of the garden just outside, comprises three distinct sections. The first highlights the savoir-faire (know-how) of Berber tribes, showcasing utensils and objects used in domestic life. In the next room, the complexities of tribal identity and social status are explored in a collection of ornaments and jewels worn by Berber women. And finally, a room showcasing the beauty of Berber craftsmanship across costumes, weapons and musical instruments ends the exhibition. Expertly curated, it is worth setting aside a chunk of time to soak in the wealth of information in this museum. Having some understanding of Berber history and culture will enhance your experience in Marrakesh.

Located inside Jardin Majorelle, Rue Yves Saint Laurent

Mon–Sun 8am–6pm

MAD

30 MAD entry

W

jardinmajorelle.com

Explore

Gallery 127

Showcasing contemporary photography from up-and-coming Moroccan and international talent.

When Gallery 127 opened in 2006, it was one of the first in Africa to focus on contemporary photography. It was founded by Nathalie Locatelli who, after a successful career in France curating exhibitions for a luxury jewellery brand, moved to Marrakesh to follow her passion: photography. Locatelli was new to the art world when she opened Gallery 127 in the heart of Guéliz/Ville Nouvelle, now the neighbourhood of choice for Marrakesh's contemporary art galleries. She now represents a unique group of photographers on an international scale, including at major events such as Paris Photo (the world's largest international art fair dedicated to photography).

The exhibitions change regularly and show a diverse collection of works from Moroccan and international photographers. Previous exhibitions have included: works by French–Moroccan photographer Carolle Benitah, in which she explored her family history, reviving old family photos by adding new elements such as hand-embroidery or gold foil; and the black and white photographs by Moroccan photographer, Safaa Mazirh, whose images capture and dramatise the movement of the human body – a subject that forms the core of her work.

127 Avenue Mohammed V	Tues–Sat 3–7pm	MAD Free

Explore

Museum of Art and Culture of Marrakesh (MACMA)

A collection of artworks by Orientalist artists that explore daily life in Morocco.

61 Rue Yougoslavie

Mon–Sat 9am–7pm

MAD

80 MAD

W

museemacma.com

Opened in 2016, MACMA is a private museum founded by art collector Nabil El Mallouki. An influential period in art history, in which artists depicted their experience and impressions of the East, Orientalist art is often criticised as having a colonial agenda, however it can also be a genuine recreation by the artists of their experience and perceptions. MACMA's permanent and rotating exhibitions explore all facets of life in Morocco, including the role of religion, the judicial system and caravanserai (trading route inns) culture, as documented by Orientalist artists from the 19th century through to the early 20th century.

Located in the 'new city' of Guéliz/ Ville Nouvelle, in a pocket of art galleries and trendy eateries (see Comptoir des Mines, p.103 and Plus 61, p.49), the museum is decidedly more modern that many of its counterparts. The space was designed by architect Amine Tounsi to enhance the presentation of and interaction with the artworks.

Comptoir des Mines

A gallery that shines a spotlight on contemporary Moroccan art.

62 Rue Yougoslavie

Mon 3–7pm
Tues–Sat 10am–1pm, 3–7pm

MAD
Free

W
comptoirdesminesgalerie.com

Formerly the office of a French mining company, Comptoir des Mines is a contemporary art gallery in the heart of Guéliz/Ville Nouvelle. The 1930s building has been transformed into a sleek space that forms a discreet backdrop for contemporary art, while retaining its Art Deco charm. The brainchild of Hicham Daoudi, a prominent figure in Marrakesh's art world, the gallery feeds a rapidly growing and global interest in African art, and has opened the doors to a new side of Marrakesh – one that looks beyond the city's history and towards a modern interpretation of Morocco's culture through contemporary art.

The gallery hosts rotating exhibitions by emerging and established artists that creatively explore and broaden the dialogue of North African culture and history. Highlights from previous exhibitions include: an installation of oversized Arabic words made from keyboard letters and electric board circuits by Larbi Cherkaoui, as well as the striking paintings of prominent Moroccan artist Mohammed Kacimi.

Explore

Museum of African Contemporary Art Al Maaden (MACAAL)

An internationally acclaimed museum
that celebrates contemporary African art.

While most of Marrakesh's historical sights and museums are within the walls of the medina, 20 minutes away in a terracotta pink building is the only museum on the African continent dedicated entirely to contemporary African art. Following a soft opening in 2016, the Museum of African Contemporary Art Al Maaden (known as MACAAL) was catapulted into the international arena when it officially opened to the public in 2018 alongside 1:54 – an international art fair dedicated to contemporary African art. While so much of Marrakesh's soul is rooted in the past, behind its ancient facade a contemporary art scene has been flourishing.

An independent non-profit initiative of Moroccan art collector Alami Lazraq and his son Othman Lazraq, the family's enviable collection of African art is brought to life here, alongside rotating exhibitions from established and emerging artists across a range of media. A striking white space, the museum was designed to mimick elements of the medina with a labyrinth-like layout – an effort to connect the museum with local life in the city. Beyond the gallery space itself, MACAAL hosts a range of educational events, as well as an artist residency – a studio and living space for emerging African artists set between the museum and the Al Maaden Sculpture Park (a collection of unique sculptures set around the neighbouring golf course).

Al Maaden, Sidi Youssef
Ben Ali

Tues–Sun 10am–6pm

MAD

70 MAD

W

macaal.org

SHOP

Marrakesh's talented artisans and enticing souks have
attracted treasure hunters from around the world for centuries.
The souks are a dizzying collection of vendors selling
everything from babouches (traditional slippers) to Berber
carpets. The souk's winding alleys are colourful, energetic and
a place to bargain; you'll undoubtedly get wonderfully lost
in the chaos. The little alleys that weave around the souks
are lined with interesting boutiques and artisans. Don't miss
the treasures within Mustapha Baloui's (see p.117) famed
homewares store or Soufiane Zarib (see p.121), the legendary
carpet-seller of Marrakesh.

By contrast with the medina, Guéliz/Ville Nouvelle offers
manicured streets, boutiques and malls with air-conditioning
and fixed price tags. In recent years the city's design scene has
flourished, led by a new generation of Moroccans and foreign
creatives who are merging the savoir-faire (know-how) of
local artisans with modern design. The barren workshops and
warehouses of the former industrial area of Sidi Ghanem
have been transformed into a hub of their contemporary
design ateliers and showrooms.

Malakut

A soulful shop creating unique ceramics and contemporary Moroccan clothing.

54 Trik Sidi Abdel Aziz

Mon–Sun 11am–1.30pm
& 2.30–7.30pm

MAD

600 MAD+

Salah-eddine Bouhiri represents the new generation of creatives who are bringing a new dimension to Moroccan artisanship, with their contemporary take on traditional crafts. In his tiny shop in the heart of the medina, one of a cluster of stores who embody a similar ideology (also see Kitan, p.114), Salah-eddine sells his range of minimalistic ceramics and unisex Moroccan clothing embroidered with Picasso-esque one-line drawings. All of his pieces are handmade in Marrakesh and alongside his own works he stocks a range of scarves made by a women's collective, giving jobs to women in need.

For Salah-eddine, his interaction with his customers is one of the most important and enjoyable aspects of his work. Despite being approached to collaborate with huge international brands, he doesn't want to industrialise his work, opting to stay small and local.

Nasire

Swiss design meets Moroccan craftsmanship in a timeless collection of leather bags.

81 Derb Nkhal Rahba Lakdima

Mon–Sun 11am–8pm

MAD

100 MAD+

W

nasire.com

Founded in 2016 by two friends Matteo Lettieri, and Michael Lütolf, Nasire takes two distinct elements from polar worlds: the strong lines of Swiss design and the vibrant colours of Morocco, to create a collection of bold, yet effortlessly minimalist leather bags. Born from an entrepreneurial spirit and a desire to travel without typical constraints, the brand carries this sentiment at its core by designing its range for the modern-day nomad.

Deviating from machine-led mass production, Nasire's bags are handmade by leather craftsmen who draw on generations of savoir-faire (know-how) to create their classic pieces. In the pared-back boutique in the heart of the medina, a collection of their everyday bags and small leather goods are displayed, made from soft leather in four key colours: cobalt blue, tan brown, white and black.

Shop

Kulchi

A treasure-trove of handmade rugs and textiles, sourced from all over Morocco.

60 Rahba derb Nkhal

By appointment, Mon–Sun
10am–7pm

MAD
500 MAD+

W
kulchi.com

The long-time business of Cassandra Karinsky, an Australian expat who has called Marrakesh home for 12 years, Kulchi (meaning 'everything' in Arabic) is the product of her love for Moroccan design. A short walk from Place des Epices (Spice Market, see p.75), Cassandra has converted a riad into a showroom for her extensive collection of vintage Berber rugs that she sources from around Morocco, as well as a range of rugs she designs with artisans in the Atlas Mountains.

Stacked in piles so high and in a myriad of styles and colours, it is impossible to navigate the selection of rugs without the help of one of Kulchi's friendly team members who will help you unfurl designs that spark your interest. In addition to the stock instore, they can also source and customise specific pieces for their clients, which can be shipped internationally. To visit Kulchi, make an appointment via email: info@kulchi.com (a few days in advance, if possible).

Max & Jan

A fashion and lifestyle hub in the heart of the medina.

14 Rue Amsefah, Sidi Abdelaziz

Mon–Sun 9am–11pm

MAD

200 MAD+

W

maxandjan.com

Named after its founders, Swiss–Belgian design duo Maximilian Scharl and Belgian Jan Pauwels, Max & Jan started as a clothing line in 2007. Since then it has expanded into a fashion and lifestyle hub occupying a sprawling multi-tiered space on one of the medina's many winding streets. At the core of their concept is Max & Jan's own label of contemporary clothing inspired by Moroccan heritage and design, with a focus on fairtrade and sustainability. The duo create two menswear and womenswear collections each year, both rooted in resortwear and defined by casual pieces like flowing dresses in lightweight fabrics, kaftans in quirky patterns and relaxed shirts.

Around their own label Max & Jan also stocks a collection of other Moroccan-based brands, across clothing, accessories and homewares. The store also boasts a rooftop restaurant, Soul Food, serving organic and locally sourced ingredients for lunch and dinner.

Shop

Riad Yima

*Celebrating the bold work of one of Morocco's
most pre-eminent artists.*

Tucked away in the medina behind Place des Epices (Spice Market, see
p.75), Riad Yima is a gallery-cum-boutique dedicated to the work of one of
Morocco's most pre-eminent contemporary artists, Hassan Hajjaj. Best known
for his photography, Hassan's work playfully challenges Western perceptions
of Moroccan culture and the influence of global capitalism. His work merges
fashion photography and pop art to create striking images of his subjects,
mainly his friends, in colourful Moroccan attire, set within frames lined
with distinct Maghrebi products.
Set in a former riad (traditional courtyard house), Riad Yima is a loud
space that embodies the spirit of Hassan's work, with its clashing prints and
bold colour. Across three rooms is a range of his original works and limited-
edition prints, amongst a quirky collection of more affordable take-home
pieces, like books, clothing and upcycled bags.

52 Derb Aarjane
Rahba lakdima

Mon–Thurs 10am–7pm
Fri 10am–1.30pm
Sat–Sun 10am–7pm

MAD

300 MAD+

W

iadyima.blogspot.com

Shop

Kitan

*Japanese design meets
Moroccan craftsmanship
in a line of clean and
contemporary clothing.*

Derb Smara Kandil no. 11, Sidi
Abdel Aziz

Mon–Fri 9.30am–12.30pm
& 2.30–6pm
Sat 9.30am–2pm

MAD
500 MAD+

On her first visit to Marrakesh in 2007, Mai Yamazk was captivated by the beauty and vitality of the city. In awe of the textiles, Mai was inspired to start a label to celebrate Morocco's ancient artisanship and Japanese design, and so Kitan was born.

Working with a team of local seamstresses, Mai draws on traditional techniques to create her own take on classic Moroccan styles. On a lively street in the medina, also where Malakut (see p.108) has set up shop, Mai's store is an airy space with dense racks full of her collections: simple and elegant pieces made with natural materials, such as cotton and raffia, and finished with touches of Moroccan embroidery.

Funky Cool Medina

A quirky shop selling vintage pieces sourced from around the world and a line of upcycled clothing.

65 Rue Sidi el Yamani
(opposite Maison du Caftan)

Mon–Sat 10am–8pm

MAD
200 MAD+

Run by three friends: Fadh, Khalid and Mohammed, Funky Cool Medina is a goldmine of unique vintage pieces and quirky clothing. The small hole-in-the-wall store in the medina is packed tightly with racks of items sourced from all over the world. Alongside their vintage selection, Fadh, Khalid and Mohammed design their own clothing, bags and hats from upcycled materials.

The trio can often be found lingering out the front of their shop, talking to other shopowners or entertaining customers. They'll happily indulge you with the history of each item and play dress-ups with you as you try on bits and bobs from their eccentric collection. Outside of Marrakesh, they can often be found on the UK festival circuit, at the likes of Glastonbury and Womad, with their pop-up store.

Shop

Amine Bendriouich

Androgynous pieces in luxurious fabrics, with stories of African heritage.

76 Blvd el Mansour Eddahbi

Mon–Sat 10am–7pm

MAD
1000 MAD+

W
amine.bendriouich.com

Founded in 2008 by Amine Bendriouich, Marrakesh's internationally celebrated designer, who simultaneously pays tribute to African culture while pushing the norms of traditional dressing with his eponymous brand. Since his first collection, the Marrakesh born-and-bred artist has been celebrated internationally for his free-spirited designs. Drawing on his cultural identity, Amine's work is anchored in his African heritage and formed by the fluidity of his self-expression. The result is a unique collection of androgynous pieces in luxurious fabrics, like cashmere, silk and linen, designed away from the realm of trend-driven fashion.

Approaching his work as a form of storytelling, each of Amine's collections has its own narrative inspired by the world around him: the birds of Ghana, the intersection of Berlin and Morocco, society's obsession with money, the costumes of Gnawa musicians (a collection he produced with pre-eminent Moroccan artist, Hassan Hajjaj, see p.113) and for his latest collection: Berber symbolism.

Mustapha Baloui

An Aladdin's cave of treasures hidden behind a discreet door in the medina.

---

144 Arset Aouzal Rd

Mon–Sun 10am–7pm

MAD

500 MAD+

By no means a hidden gem, but a gem nonetheless, Mustapha Baloui is a popular Marrakesh spot for interior designers from all over the world and anyone in-the-know looking for homewares. The store takes the name of its owner, Mustapha, who has packed every inch of his cave-like space with artisanal homewares sourced from Morocco and other African countries. He's endlessly interesting and full of stories about the items he collects and, if you're lucky, he'll be there to guide you through his maze of unique pieces.

Starting on the ground floor, where rugs and textiles are stacked high under a sky of Moroccan lanterns, the store then morphs across several floors into a labyrinth of furniture, antiques, ceramics, silverware, mirrors and more. Truly an Aladdin's cave, each nook is filled with unique treasures. It is hard to walk away empty-handed and anything too big to fit in your suitcase can be shipped internationally.

Shop

Laly

*The label updating traditional Moroccan dressing
with a contemporary take on classic styles.*

Badra Bengeloune has updated Moroccan dressing for the modern-day woman
with her label Laly. Badra's personal style is fun and vibrant – characteristics
that are embedded in her playful approach with Laly, using vibrant colours
and bold prints to freshen up traditional Moroccan womenswear. All her
garments and accessories are made locally with fabric that she sources from
around the world. With two locations in the medina, one on an arterial path
between Jemaa el-Fnaa (see p.71) and the kasbah (the most ancient part
of the medina), and the other in the busy pocket of the west medina, Laly's
boutiques are chic and intimate spaces with friendly staff who will talk you
through the background of each piece.

Designed for warm climates, Laly's collections are characterised
by flowing dresses and loose-fitting garments in luxurious lightweight
fabrics, such as silk and linen. Relaxed yet elevated, each piece discreetly
nods to traditional Moroccan dressing, whether it be in the shape, a touch of
embroidery or a tassel tucked under the collar.

		MAD
137 Dar Bâcha	Mon–Sun 9.30am–8pm	1500 MAD+
(west medina)		
104 Hay Elkennaria		
Essouika (kasbah,		
south medina)		

Shop

Soufiane Zarib

The carpet legend of Marrakesh.

It's not possible to talk about carpets in Marrakesh without talking about Soufiane Zarib. Carpets have been in his family for generations, but Soufiane has taken the family business to new heights with his modern approach to the trade. He has a global reputation as Marrakesh's go-to carpet dealer and has a great eye. Over the years, Soufiane has built a carpet empire with several stores across the city and has since expanded into homewares.

His main showroom is a multi-tiered space hidden behind a fort-like door in the west of the medina. It is a must-stop destination for anyone interested in buying homewares in Marrakesh. A ring of the doorbell and a heavy wooden door will open to reveal stacks and stacks of Moroccan carpets piled high on the ground floor, each layer hinting at what lies within the folded pieces. Soufiane and his team will happily help you discover their collection of rugs, effortlessly pulling them from the piles and unfolding them in the large, open space to reveal stunning pieces in rich colours and designs. They will indulge you with stories of their origins and the meaning of the symbolism and colours of each rug, while you sip sweet mint tea. Be sure to wander upstairs to explore a more refined space styled with furniture and homewares.

16 Rue Riad Laarous	8.30am–7.30pm	MAD
		5000 MAD+

W

soufiane-zarib.com

Shop

33 Majorelle

Marrakesh's pre-eminent concept store stocking a range of Moroccan brands.

A stone's throw away from the Jardin Majorelle (see p.97) and the Yves Saint Laurent Museum (see p.95), 33 Majorelle is the city's go-to destination for the latest in fashion, accessories and homewares. One of the only concept stores in Marrakesh, it brings together some of the best Moroccan brands under one roof.

Across the two floors in the sprawling and airy space, is a well curated selection from established and up-and-coming Moroccan designers and artisans, such as Laly's (see p.119) beautiful flowing dresses and the fashion world's favourite handcrafted babouches (Moroccan slippers) from Zyne.

33 Rue Yves Saint Laurent

Mon–Sun 9am–7pm

MAD
300 MAD+

W
33ruemajorelle.com

Kaftan Queen

The fashion-forward label making the modern-day Moroccan wardrobe.

61 Rue Yugoslavie,
39-41 Passage Ghandouri

Mon–Sat 10am–7pm

MAD
300 MAD+

W
kaftanqueen.store

The brainchild of Brit-expat and former model-turned-designer and entrepreneur, Sarah Rouach, Kaftan Queen has become the first choice for modern Moroccan fashion. In her on-site atelier under Kaftan Queen's boutique in Guéliz/Ville Nouvelle, nestled amongst contemporary galleries and studios, Sarah works with her team of tailors to produce her designs, which are inspired by traditional Moroccan dresses. Upstairs in the boutique, glamourous kaftans and flowing garments, made with locally sourced fabrics and finished with touches of embroidery in rich colours, line the bright white walls.

If the sizing isn't right, Sarah offers personal tailoring at no extra cost. Kaftan Queen's range also includes decorated babouches (Moroccan slippers), oversized clutches, bags and jewellery. Kaftan Queen also has a second location in the medina at 186 Ave El Fetouakai, Arset Lamaach (across from the entrance to the Bab Mellah Mosque).

Shop

Maison ARTC

*Fashion meets art at this unique boutique, with
one-of-a-kind pieces crafted from upcycled materials.*

Founder and designer Artsi Ifrash is daring, unapologetically outspoken
and fiercely proud to call himself Moroccan, all qualities that form the core
of this brand. In a discreet apartment block in Guéliz/Ville Nouvelle, he has
created his own eccentric world in which he reinvents Moroccan dressing
and challenges the notion of fashion. Maison ARTC's ethos is deeply rooted
in respecting and preserving Moroccan culture and craftsmanship, while
celebrating individualism and practicing sustainability.

A self-taught designer, Artsi approaches his clothing with an
unrestricted and adventurous spirit that speaks both to the past and present.
The result: beautifully crafted collections made from upcycled materials sourced
from around the world and defined by exaggerated silhouettes, eccentric fabrics
and bold colours. In using vintage fabrics, Artsi views his clothes as reviving
memories, giving the fabric new life in the form of his avant-garde designs.
His boutique is lined with head-turning dresses, flowing blouses and playful
pants. Together with Moroccan, Belgium-based photographer Mous Lamrabat,
the pair create striking images that feature Artsi's designs and are inspired
by Moroccan culture, as perceived through their unique lens. Maison ARTC is
a must-visit.

---

96 Rue Mohammed   Mon–Sun 11am–8pm   **MAD**
el Beqal   3000 MAD+

                                            W
                                    maisonartc.com

Shop

Some

A collection of Moroccan pieces from local designers.

---

76 Boulevard el Mansour Eddahbi

Mon–Sat 10am–7pm

MAD
100 MAD+

Set in a dusty pink villa in Guéliz/Ville Nouvelle, in a pocket of art galleries and restaurants (including Comptoir des Mines, see p.103 and Grand Café de La Poste, see p.52). Some stocks a range of contemporary Moroccan homewares. Founded by two French designers, Mathilde and Noémie, the duo has curated a collection of beautiful objects from both established and emerging local designers.

Each room of the villa lends itself to a different range of products. On the ground floor, chic hand-painted ceramics and Moroccan tea glasses and other glassware, are intermingled with furniture and accessories. There's a 'basket bar', offering a selection of French market-style baskets with customisable leather straps. Upstairs, in the villa's former kitchen, is a mini pantry stocked with non-perishable local gourmet items and on the last floor, a collection of Berber rugs sourced from all around Morocco.

Chabi Chic

A modern approach to Moroccan ceramics.

Arguably one of the most well-known ceramicists in Marrakesh, Chabi Chic was founded in 2013 by Vanessa Di Mino and Nadia Noël and has since grown into a coveted lifestyle brand, with a network of several stores and international stockists. The French duo draw inspiration from traditional Moroccan ceramics to create a contemporary collection of homewares, all handmade in Morocco.

322 main street, Sidi Ghanem

Mon–Sat 9.30am–1pm
& 2–7.30pm

MAD
200 MAD+

W
chabi-chic.com

Chabi Chic's flagship store, a large warehouse-like space in Marrakesh's industrial area Sidi Ghanem, has shelves stacked high with vases, bowls, plates and cups, all handpainted in Chabi Chic's signature pastel patterns. See Chabi Chic's website for more locations in the medina.

Shop

Marrakshi Life

*The cult label reviving traditional techniques
to create the modern Marrakeshi uniform.*

Founded in 2013 by New York fashion photographer, Randall Bachner, Marrakshi Life celebrates slow fashion. Randall represents a new guard of designers in the Red City, bringing traditional Moroccan design and craftsmanship into the modern era. Based on traditional Moroccan pieces and updated for modern-day-life, each garment is made from hand-loomed fabric produced by a team of Moroccan artisans. The entire production process takes place in Randall's atelier in Marrakesh's industrial area, Sidi Ghanem, where a group of local weavers and tailors draw from ancient techniques to create a modern Marrakeshi uniform. Each of Randall's androgynous collections are inspired by traditional Moroccan styles and updated with a contemporary touch. He is also committed to zero waste, turning off-cuts into patchwork life-pieces.

Next door to the workspace, the finished pieces hang in a collection of pastel colourways: lightweight and easy-to-wear unisex jumpsuits, shirts and pants, along with more structured pieces like boxy blazers and trench coats. Marrakshi Life is also stocked at Max & Jan (see p.111) and in El Fenn boutique (see p.155), but heading out to Randall's boutique and atelier (about a 20-minute drive from the medina) to experience the brand in full is well worth the taxi drive.

      MAD

933 Quartier Industriel Al   Mon–Fri 9am–5pm   2000 MAD+
Massar, Route de Safi   (closed Friday 1.30–3pm
for prayer)   **W**

marrakshilife.com

Shop

Topolina

*Flowing silhouettes
meet quirky designs
and bold colours at
this playful boutique.*

368, Sidi Ghanem

Mon–Sat 10am– 8pm

MAD
1000 MAD+

W
topolina.shop

French patternmaker Isabelle Lallemang, aka Topolina, has created a world of eccentric and bold designs with her eponymous brand. After a career in hospitality as a restaurateur and guesthouse owner in France, Isabelle pivoted into fashion when she left France for Marrakesh in 2010. What started as a small venture has now morphed into a coveted label, defined by clashing prints, bold colours and flowing silhouettes.

Handmade in Morocco, Isabelle produces her pieces with new and vintage fabrics that she sources from all around Africa. Her label started with womenswear, but Isabelle now works alongside her son Pierre-Henry, who heads up their menswear collection of relaxed clothing and bold loafers. Topolina has a few locations around Marrakesh but their flagship store is located in Sidi Ghanem. On entering the boutique, the bleakness of the industrial area immediately falls away, and brightly coloured walls and an overload of patterns quickly transport you into the world of Topolina.

Le Magasin Général

20th-century furniture and homewares, with French provincial style.

369 Route de Safi, Sidi Ghanem

Mon–Fri 9.30am–12.30pm
& 2.30–6pm
Sat 9.30am–2pm

MAD
500 MAD+

W
magasin-general-marrakech.
com

Despite being located in Marrakesh's industrial zone, Sidi Ghanem, once you walk through the doors of this charming store, the dusty streets transform into a bucolic setting. Opened by Delphine Mottet and Jean-François, a Belgian couple with a background in interior design, Le Magasin Général (the general store in French) stocks a wide range of provincial-style furniture and homewares in its sprawling warehouse-like space.

Specialising in vintage pieces, Delphine and Jean-François have curated a beautiful and ever-changing collection of 20th-century furniture, wicker chairs, dainty glassware and posters, as well as smaller items that will fit in your suitcase like candles and linens. Le Magasin Général can arrange international shipping for larger items too.

Shop

LRNCE

A coveted lifestyle brand, with a distinct
collection of homewares.

In the heart of Marrakesh's industrial district, Sidi Ghanem, LRNCE is renowned for its quirky homewares. Founded in 2013 by Belgian designer, Laurence Leenaert, her ceramics and textiles are some of the most coveted products coming out of the Red City. LRNCE's (pronounced Laurence) light-filled studio and showroom is a blissful place filled with Laurence's colourful designs, all handmade in Marrakesh by local artisans. Laurence draws inspiration from African tribes and the beauty in her daily life in Marrakesh to create contemporary pieces that nod to North African heritage.

Characterised by Picasso and Miró-like motifs in vivid colours, Laurence's ceramics are handmade with terracotta clay and then glazed, giving them a grounded and earthy, yet polished, feel. Over the years her range has expanded and now includes clothing, shoes, bags and a limited collection of furniture alongside her ceramics and textiles. A short drive from the medina, LRNCE is a must-visit for any homeware enthusiast. Note that the street doesn't have a name and finding the location of 59 Marrakesh is challenging. Taking a taxi is your best bet.

59 Marrakesh

Mon–Fri 2.15–6.30pm
Sat 10am–1pm

MAD

500 MAD+

W

lrnce.com

Shop

RELAX

There is no better way to unwind in the Red City than with a visit to a hammam. One of the oldest bathing traditions in the world, the term hammam describes the bathhouse but it is also the bathing ritual itself, which involves spending some time in a heated area to relax the body and open pores, before a rigorous body scrub using black olive oil soap known as savon beldi.

There are two distinct kinds of hammam in Marrakesh: public and private. Public hammams are shared bathing spaces, segregated by gender, where attendees bring their own supplies (from soap to a bucket for scooping water). A cornerstone of daily life, they are as much about the social aspect as they are about the bathing, but can be overwhelming for first-timers. In contrast, private hammams are akin to modern-day spas. From the uber-luxe experience at iconic La Mamounia (see p.141) to the more affordable Hammam de la Rose (see p.137), here you will find a tightly curated list of private hammams.

Le Bains de Tarabel

A discreet spa with an elevated take on the traditional hammam.

8 Derb Sraghna

By appointment

MAD

500 MAD+

W

riad-de-tarabel.com/spa

Part of the tasteful boutique hotel Riad Tarabel (see p.145), this spa is accessible through a secret door in the courtyard for hotel guests, and by an independent street entrance adjacent to the hotel for non-staying guests. Flooded with natural light and delightful aromas, Le Bains de Tarabel is a sanctuary of relaxation amidst the bustling medina. The spa has the same elegant DNA as the hotel, with a chic interior complemented by a palette of calming colours.

Treatments include a range of massages and facials, using exclusive organic products from Moroccan brand Nectarome. Bookings are generously spaced out, so it is rare that two people will be in the common areas of the spa at the same time, giving each guest their own private experience here.

Hammam de la Rose

An affordable hammam experience without compromising on quality.

130 Dar El Bacha

By appointment

MAD
250 MAD

W
hammamdelarose.com

Outside of the city's high-end spa options, there are only a handful of more affordable spas that are truly up to standard, and Hammam de la Rose is one of them. An impeccably clean spa with professional and friendly staff, it offers a high-end service without the price tag. It is set across two levels and the decor leans more traditional than modern, with hammam treatment rooms decked out in mesmerising green zellige (mosaic tiles). The spa offers a variety of different treatments, however the traditional hammam experience is where it excels.

Found on a lively street on the cusp of the souks in the medina and minutes from an arterial road (Avenue El Glaoui) that winds around the core of the medina, the location makes Hammam de la Rose the perfect place to end a day exploring. Taxis will arrive within minutes of your treatment, helping to preserve your state of bliss while you make your way back to your accommodation.

Relax

Farnatchi Spa

A luxury spa offering a high-end, yet affordable hammam experience.

60 Souk Ahl Fes

By appointment

MAD
350 MAD

W
farnatchispa.com

Ideally located behind a discreet door in the heart of the medina, Farnatchi Spa subtly merges traditional Moroccan features with contemporary design. Inside, a crisp and light interior featuring intricate woodwork is married with black and white checkered marble and a neutral colour palette to create elegant decor. Part of the five-star boutique hotel by the same name, Farnatchi Spa follows in the same luxurious footsteps as the hotel but without a five-star price tag. The prices are extremely reasonable for the high-quality service and plush environment. The classic hammam is priced at only 100 MAD more than the lowest prices found in the medina, but the jump in standard measures well beyond that.

It offers a range of other treatments, including facials, massages and manicures using all natural Moroccan products from their partners, Nectarome and ILA.

Royal Mansour Spa

This decidedly elegant spa is the epitome of luxury.

Rue Abou Abbas El Sebti

By appointment

MAD
1400 MAD+

W
royalmansour.com/en

As part of Marrakesh's most luxurious property, the Royal Mansour Spa maintains an impeccable reputation for being one of the most indulgent spa experiences in the city. An all-white sanctuary, soaring ceilings and the immaculate decor elicit a sense of Zen immediately on entering. The hotel itself is owned by Morocco's King Mohammed VI, who spared no expense in commissioning over 1000 artisans to create an extraordinarily luxurious property and the spa is no exception.

Royal Mansour's signature hammam is a contemporary take on the traditional hammam, and individually tailored for each guest. For the ultimate spa experience, opt for a treatment in one of three spa suites: secluded rooms with their own treatment area, plunge pool and private terrace. As to be expected at a spa of this calibre, prices run high but are worth every penny.

Relax

La Mamounia

Nestled within a fabled historical hotel,
this spa is a lavish hideaway.

A prestigious hotel dating back to 1923, La Mamounia was once a favourite of Winston Churchill and has welcomed a long list of world leaders, acclaimed artists and movie stars to its exceptional property. The hotel has long been a beacon of luxury in Marrakesh and its spa follows suit. Despite its cachet, guests are warmly welcomed into the opulent oasis, which boasts an elaborate list of treatments: from high-end hammams and indulgent massages, to hair and nail care.

La Mamounia offers a day pass that includes a hammam or massage at the spa, access to its pools – a stunning indoor one framed by horseshoe arches decorated with zellige (mosaic tiles) and intricate woodwork, it is perhaps one of the most Instagrammed pools in Marrakesh – and a sprawling outdoor pool shaded by towering palm trees. It is all topped off with a lunch of fresh salads and flavoursome pastas at La Mamounia's Mediterranean restaurant, Le Pavillon de la Piscine. Lunch is great value at 1500 MAD (considering treatments start at 1200 MAD), and it's the perfect option during summer months when temperatures soar too high for sightseeing. Alternatively, couple a late-afternoon treatment with a sunset and cocktail on the terrace overlooking La Mamounia's sprawling gardens, which are home to over 900 trees and 5000 rose bushes, and linger in the luxury as an orange glow engulfs the stunning grounds.

The hotel is undergoing renovations, re-opening September 2020 following a major refurbishment.

Avenue Bab Jdid

By appointment

MAD

1200 MAD+

W

mamounia.com

STAY

When it comes to where to stay in Marrakesh, the city offers three distinct areas: the ancient medina, the more modern Hivernage that boasts famed luxury hotels frequented by the jet-set crowd, and a few kilometres further north, the Palmeraie, a palm tree grove oasis, favoured by those looking to relax in its sprawling five-star resorts, luxury private villas and upscale golf courses.

For the most authentic experience, there is no other place to stay than in the atmospheric medina. Its winding maze-like streets are full of riads: traditional Moroccan family homes, characterised by open-air interior courtyards, which have been converted into charming guesthouses and luxury boutique hotels. Often owned and run by expats, some riads embrace typical Moroccan styles, while others marry contemporary design with traditional architecture. Riads tend to be intimate properties, hosting only a handful of guests. Each property in this chapter has something special to offer: unparalleled style, a panoramic rooftop or impeccable service.

Riad Tarabel

*An elegant boutique hotel that
exudes old-world charm.*

A colonial-style mansion turned boutique hotel, Riad Tarabel is a luxurious getaway with an abundance of style, offering a first-class experience but without a hint of pretentiousness. The riad started out as a private retreat for its owners Leonard Degoy and Rose Marie Fournier. Over the years, by acquiring and joining neighbouring properties, the couple turned it into a boutique hotel, with 10 relaxed, yet sophisticated, rooms, and generous suites with stunning bathrooms: the junior suite has two deep freestanding baths, perfect to soak in after a long day in the medina. There is also an eight-metre pool, relaxed rooftop and a lush spa (see p.136) hidden behind a mirror-cum-door in the central courtyard.

   An elegant mix of design, the Moroccan architecture here plays backdrop to French colonial interiors, accented by a colour scheme of muted olive, cream and black shades. There is a sense of romance and nostalgia threaded through the decor, with antiques from all over the world and family heirlooms from Leonard's château in France dotted throughout. A decidedly discreet property, photos of Riad Tarabel are rarely found splashed across social media, giving the hotel a private aura. The tasteful property is bolstered by hospitable French manager Laurent Bocca and an impeccable team of staff, for whom no ask is too big.

          MAD

8 Derb Sraghna   4 stars   2500 MAD

W

riad-de-tarabel.com

Stay

Zwin Zwin Hotel & Spa

A lively hotel and spa with unbeatable views from its rooftop terrace.

---

10 Rue El Moustachfa

3 stars

MAD

700 MAD

W

zwinzwin.com

Opened by savvy French woman Natalie Rousseau, previously of Zwin Zwin cafe in the medina, she shut her beloved eatery for broader horizons, opening a hotel and spa by the same name in 2019. Well located within easy reach of Jemaa el-Fnaa (see p.71) and other key attractions (El Badi Palace, see p.91 and the Saadian Tombs, see p.89, are 10 minutes away), Zwin Zwin is a lively 13-bedroom property with a traditional hammam (bathhouse) on its ground floor. Affordably priced, there aren't many other properties in the city that offer the comparable quality at the same rates. Crisply decorated in a simple fashion, rooms are unfussy and provide standard comforts.

 Upstairs, decked out in a navy blue and white colour scheme, the two-tiered rooftop terrace is a real highlight, where there is an updated version of Zwin Zwin cafe that is open to non-guests. Boasting unparalleled panoramic views of the medina's rooftops and towering minarets, it is one of the highest rooftops in the city. The central staircase services the whole property, so foot traffic passing the guestrooms from cafe-goers is to be expected.

Riad Emberiza

An elegant riad with a serene internal courtyard and impeccable hospitality.

23 Derb Khoshba
Zaouia Abbassia

4 stars

MAD
2000 MAD

W
riademberizasahari.com

A true Marrakesh gem, Riad Emberiza is one of the city's best-kept secrets. Among the hordes of riads, it stands out as one of the most beautiful. A unique property for its stunning architecture and design, there is no better place to retire to after a day exploring the medina. Rarely splashed over social media, it remains a well-guarded secret of those in-the-know. An intimate and luxurious riad, it has only six rooms, each individually decorated with a chic and minimalist take on Moroccan design. Towering arches and long balconies frame the light-filled courtyard, home to an inviting pool surrounded by orange and lemon trees, under which a generous Moroccan-style breakfast is served each morning.

At the end of a lively street lined with food vendors in the north of the medina, Riad Emberiza's location is refreshingly local and within a short walk of key attractions. At the heart of the riad is its owner, Alexandra Richards – an Australian expat who has called Marrakesh home for over a decade – who exudes a genuine hospitality that makes her property feel more like a family home.

Stay

Riad 42

A chic fusion of contemporary design with traditional architecture.

📍

42 Derb lalla Azouna

✳

4 stars

MAD

1000 MAD

Riad 42 is an elegant, minimalist bolthole and a far cry from the typical style of riad found in Marrakesh, with a sense of space not often found in such crammed quarters of the city. It is buried down a labyrinth in the medina but near some of the key attractions (Maison de la Photographie, see p.79; Medersa Ben Youssef, see p.77; and Musée de la Femme, see p.81).

Owners French–Belgian couple, Sarah and Grégoire Rasson, have opted for a pared-back approach to interiors, leaving the stunning architecture of their riad to take centrestage. The property boasts an abundance of light, with soaring ceilings and an all-white interior that create a calming backdrop to return to after a day in the chaotic medina. Deep Moroccan lounges invite weary explorers to unwind with a mint tea and the rooftop beckons with beautiful sunset views. To book, email Sarah at theriad42@gmail.com.

Riad L'atelier

An inspired property marrying contemporary design with Moroccan hospitality.

33 Rue Tachenbacht

4 stars

MAD
1300 MAD

W
riadlatelier.com

Superbly located, Riad L'Atelier sits on the heel of a lively local marketplace and is just minutes away from many interesting attractions (Maison de la Photographie, see p.79; Medersa Ben Youssef, see p.77 and Musée de la Femme, see p.81). Despite its busy location, once past the front door the atmosphere switches from chaotic to calm.

Stylish and contemporary are watchwords here. The riad's five light-filled rooms are uncrowded, giving space for the unique objects and vintage furniture collected from antique markets in Marrakesh and beyond, to breathe. Underfoot, sleek tadelakt flooring topped with plush Berber rugs continue seamlessly into the simple yet luxurious bathrooms. Owners Julia Rodriguez and Mauro Martínez Cubillo are involved in every aspect of the property and are a positively friendly pair, so that visitors routinely arrive as guests and leave as their friends.

Stay

La Sultana

*In the heart of the historic kasbah, this museum-like
hotel has a wealth of history.*

With an enviable location in the kasbah (the most ancient part of the medina) and just metres away from the Saadian Tombs (see p.89), La Sultana is a luxury boutique property and a stunning example of Moroccan craftsmanship and hospitality. The hotel's setting is lively but once on the other side of La Sultana's towering earthy walls, the buzz of the streets falls away and the surrounds become lush and blissfully quiet. It was created by adjoining and restoring five neighbouring riads (traditional courtyard houses). The original zellige (mosaic tiles) and cedar woodwork of the original properties have been retained, making a museum-like hotel where every corner has a detail to be admired.

Each of the 28 rooms is individually decorated in rich colours with deep wooden furnishings, yet connected by the opulent thread that ties the multi-riad property together. La Sultana boasts two pools, one in the internal courtyard and another on its sprawling rooftop garden, along with beautiful views of the neighbouring area. One of the most luxurious features of the hotel is its pink marble spa, a secluded and tranquil space offering traditional Moroccan hammams and treatments. It is accessible by non-hotel guests by reservation.

403 Rue de La Kasbah

5 stars

MAD

4000 MAD per night

W

lasultanahotels.com

Stay

L'Hôtel Marrakech

An updated 19th-century riad and a beacon
of luxury in the heart of the medina.

The first hotel of Jasper Conran, the renowned British designer behind his namesake label, L'Hôtel Marrakech embodies his good taste and effortlessly chic ethos. For his first foray as a hotelier, Jasper Conran chose an historic 19th-century riad down a winding street in a lively pocket of the medina. Previously the central part of a palace, the property was restored and re-birthed in 2016 as a luxury riad with five elegant light-filled suites, each with four-poster beds draped in crisp white linens. Flawlessly designed, the interiors subtly nod to the grandeur of the 1930s, mixing updated Moroccan interiors with contemporary textiles, antique pieces, art from Conran's private collection and pieces acquired from the collection of Yves Saint Laurent.

Despite its central location on the edge of a busy marketplace, L'Hôtel is an oasis of calm. Whether it be on a lounge chair next to the shaded saltwater pool in the courtyard garden, indulging in a Moroccan breakfast on your private balcony, among the pungent jasmine flowers, watching the sunset on the rooftop terrace or a night-cap at the zinc-topped bar in the plush lounge, the riad offers guests ample spaces to relax and unwind. All of it is topped off with impeccable service overseen by hotel manager Luca Ravera, a charming Italian who personifies the warm hospitality L'Hôtel Marrakech is so often praised for.

41 Derb Sidi Lahcen O Ali

4 stars

MAD
4500 MAD

W
l-hotelmarrakech.com

Stay

Riad BE Marrakech

An authentic riad embracing traditional Moroccan style.

---

3 Derb Sidi Lahcen O Ali

4 stars

MAD

1300 MAD

W

be-marrakech.com

In the west of the medina, in a pocket dense with guesthouses, Riad BE Marrakech offers a contemporary riad experience, while maintaining its traditional style and retro interior. A dizzying array of zellige (mosaic tiles) have been paired with bold colours, greenery and modern touches to create a photogenic interior that Instagrammers have been unable to resist. Despite the hype, it remains an intimate property with an authentic ambience.

With 10 rooms, it has the atmosphere of a family home that is perpetuated by its owners Mohammed and Nicole, and their hospitable staff. The gem of the property is its rooftop terrace: a spacious area with dramatic hessian canopies, inviting Moroccan-style lounges and towering cacti set against pastel orange walls. The duo expanded their property in 2019 to include a yoga studio, the first to open in the medina and an added benefit for the mindful traveller.

El Fenn

A coveted hotel celebrated for its bold design and relaxed take on luxury.

---

2 Derb Moulay Abdullah Ben Hezzian

4 stars

MAD
4000 MAD per night

W
el-fenn.com

Just minutes away from Jemaa el-Fnaa (see p.71), El Fenn is a coveted boutique hotel with 28 individually decorated rooms, a sprawling rooftop terrace, shaded pools, and a high-end hammam (bathhouse). Translating to 'house of art' in Arabic, the hotel doubles as a living gallery, with contemporary art hung in the deep fuchsia corridors and dotted throughout the rooms. The art is constantly changing and so too is the hotel itself.

El Fenn started its life in 2002 after Vanessa Branson and Howell James purchased the run-down riad two years earlier. As part of a refurbishment programme in 2012, general manager and interior designer Willem Smit elevated the property with his bold and eccentric approach to design. Continually expanding with new rooms, pools and terraces, no two visits to El Fenn are the same. While there are private nooks accessible by guests only, the restaurant, small contemporary boutique and rooftop bar (see p.44) are open to the public.

Stay

Dar El Sadaka

A delightfully eccentric and unique luxury villa.

Dar El Sadaka invites guests into the whimsical world of French visual artist Jean-François Forte. Located in the heart of the Palmeraie, just 15 minutes' drive from the medina, with a giant sculpture of a giraffe nibbling fresh flowers off the dining room table and life-like chimpanzees swinging across the living room, this is no ordinary property. The captivating 25-acre estate is a world of its own. With nine individually themed rooms, whether it be the tortoise suite or the bee bedroom, each takes guests to a different part of the endearing universe of Jean-François Forte in a luxurious setting. Throughout the villa and the sprawling grounds, Jean-François Forte sculptures and artwork feature prominently. From the House Fallen from the Sky, the artist's recreation of his childhood home designed to scale but upside-down, to the Giant's House (his daughter's childhood bedroom in giant proportions), Dar El Sadaka is full of surprises.

The villa is only available for private hire in its entirety (rooms cannot be booked individually and there are minimum night stays), however non-guests can still experience the property with a private lunch at the Giant's House, where the setting and food follow the artist's vision and everything is super-sized, or for sunset drinks paired with a tour of the House Fallen from the Sky. Contact Dar Sadaka through its website for more information and pricing.

---

8 Rue de Bab Aylan

5 stars

MAD

3400-3900 MAD
per night
(min. 3–7 night stay)

W

darelsadaka.com

Stay

Nicknamed the Windy City, this charming seaside town on the Atlantic Coast is famed for its picturesque blue and white medina, vibrant port, ramparts and animated fisherman. Unlike chaotic Marrakesh, life moves slower in Essaouira's charming streets lined with galleries and boutiques.

Start your day in the port where Essaouira's iconic blue boats bob in the water and wizened fishermen go about their day's work at the fish market. From there, wander up through **Bab al Mersa** (door of the port) to soak in the activity of the main square, **Place Moulay Hassan**, with a coffee at **Café Dolcefreddo**.

Then wander up Avenue Oqba Ibn Nafiaa, the medina's central vein linking Place Moulay Hassan to Essaouira's northern gate, **Bab Doukkala**. Explore the small alleyways and paths, dense with art galleries and boutiques that criss-cross off the main street. Stop at **Boheme of Morocco** (BP423 Place Al Khaima) for Moroccan homewares, **Rafia Craft** (82 Rue d'Agadir) for handmade leather and raffia accessories, and **Elizir Gallery** (22 Ave d'Istiqlal), a treasure-trove of vintage furniture.

Once you've worked up an appetite for lunch, head to **Vague Bleu** (Rue Sidi Ali Ben Abdellah), a charming six table, family-run restaurant in a small alley in the medina. Choose from the small and incredibly affordable menu of pasta cooked with fresh seafood; if you're in luck, lobster lasagne will be on the menu but it depends on the day's catch, and if the fisherman don't go out that day, then fish won't be on the menu. Watch local life go by the restaurant front as you tuck into hearty home cooking.

Walk off lunch along the **city's ramparts** (accessible from rue Skala). Constructed in the 18th century to fortify the city against invasions, they offer a stunning ocean vista and views of the medina. Stop at **Galerie d'Art Damgaard** (Avenue Oqba Ibn Nafiaa) and **Galerie du Sud** (2 Rue Laalouj) to check out the work of local artists. Spend the rest of the afternoon wandering freely through Essaouira's charming alleys – you can't take a wrong turn.

End the day with a sundowner on the rooftop at **Taros** (Place Moulay Hassan), a beloved local establishment with views of the port.

GETTING THERE

Essaouira is 191 kilometres (118 miles) and approximately a 2.5 to 3-hour drive from Marrakesh, depending on traffic. There are two options to travel by: bus or private car. A daytrip is possible with an early start, otherwise, opt to stay overnight to soak in the seaside vibe.

By car: A private driver costs around 1000 MAD return. Most riads can organise this for you, or book via websites such as: viator.com and mydaytrip.com.

By bus: The main bus company, **Supratours**, run five buses a day from its station next to the Marrakesh train station in Guéliz Ville Nouvelle (Avenue Hassan II). Tickets can be purchased online via its website for 180 MAD return. See: oncf-voyages.ma.

Daytrip

An endless moon-like plain of hardened rocky red earth and rolling dunes set against the snow-capped Atlas Mountains, the Afagay Desert is a serene oasis less than an hour away from Marrakesh. Nestled in the heart of its vast expanse, Scarabeo Camp offers an opportunity to soak in the dazzling desert scenery in a luxurious setting.

A virtually untouched part of the country, the Afagay Desert is an immense and calm oasis. Unlike the famed Sahara Desert, which is over eight hours from the Red City, the Afagay is favoured as the closer alternative for an equally exotic experience. Perched on a hill with nothing but the endless desert landscape in sight, Scarabeo Camp offers an intimate site with only 15 glamourous tents that rival many of the high-end hotels in Marrakesh – it's glamping at its finest. The white bell-style tents with lush interiors evoke an era of old-world travel glamour, each with a suite of luxurious comforts: plush beds, ensuite bathrooms, traditional Moroccan lounges, writing desks and private terraces.

There's endless opportunity for adventure activities, whether it be an exploratory mountain trek and picnic in picturesque surrounds, a thrilling quad-bike tour, a relaxing massage or a camel ride across the sun-baked terrain. Come dusk, guests are ushered outside to sink into lounges and chairs, or to huddle around flickering fires in winter months, and sip mint tea as the orange hues of the Afagay turn to a pastel swirl, while the moon replaces the sun. There is no more enchanting time of day in the desert than dusk. Once night falls, the lavish dining room comes alive when a traditional Moroccan dinner, using seasonal vegetables and accompanied by fresh-baked bread from the onsite earthen oven, is served at a candle-lit communal table.

You can stay overnight in one of the luxurious tents or simply visit the camp for the day. If you opt for a daytrip, book ahead for activities, plan to arrive early afternoon and pair a desert activity with sunset and dinner at the camp before returning to Marrakesh. Temperatures in the Afagay soar in summer months, so the cooler months of autumn, winter and early spring are the best time to visit.

GETTING THERE

Only 35 kilometres (22 miles) and less than an hour's drive from Marrakesh, the Afagay Desert is easily accessed by car. Scarabeo Camp can organise transfers on your behalf for a cost of 550 MAD each way. Alternatively, most riads in Marrakesh will happily assist you in organising a private driver if you prefer your own transport, just be sure to request a 4x4 as most other cars don't fare well on the bumpy ride.

Daytrip

A rustic, charming outpost on the outskirts of Marrakesh, this is a modern Moroccan take on the traditional country club. With several pools, a luxury spa, a fragrant rose garden and Moroccan and Mediterranean restaurants, Beldi Country Club provides respite from the dizzying streets of the Red City and is the perfect setting in which to unwind.

Just a 20-minute drive away from the medina yet a world away, there is not a hint of stress at Beldi Country Club. The intense sounds and chaos of the city are swapped for the slow pace of a bucolic lifestyle. With multi-hectare grounds, there is no rhyme or reason to the layout, wandering Beldi Country Club's winding paths feels like an adventure in itself; at every turn there's something new to be discovered. A seriously relaxing setting, across the sprawling property, travellers and locals can be found lounging by the pools, indulging at the spa, wandering through one of the many fragrant gardens or long-lunching at the poolside restaurant.

On entering the club, a short walk down an olive tree-lined path leads you to an inviting elongated pool and a shaded outdoor restaurant, tucked behind them is a second pool surrounded by sunlounges. Back-around by the entrance you'll find Beldi's take on the modern souk – a concept store stocking Moroccan carpets, embroidery and ceramics alongside contemporary resortwear. On the opposite side of the property, past the spa and tucked behind the rose garden is a 38-suite hotel, complete with its own restaurant and private pools for hotel guests, and several event spaces used for weddings and other festivities. In true country club style, Beldi offers a range of activities from golf, cooking lessons and poolside pétanque to pottery courses for kids.

Beldi Country Club has a number of day packages to choose from: access to the property, a sunlounge, towel and lunch at the poolside restaurant from the seasonal Moroccan and Mediterranean menus costs 390 MAD for adults and 250 MAD for children, or without lunch it's 200 MAD for adults and 100 MAD for children. Reservations can be made via phone or email and are essential, especially in peak-season. See: beldicountryclub.com/en for booking and more information.

GETTING THERE

Less than 10 kilometres (6 miles) from the medina, Beldi Country Club (Route du Barrage, Cherifia, Marrakesh) is only a 20-minute taxi drive from the heart of the city. All drivers will know the property by name and you can expect to pay 50–100 MAD one way. For the return journey, there are usually taxis lingering outside, however they often charge a premium, so it's best to arrange for the taxi that drops you off to also collect you at an agreed price and time.

Daytrip

A lush valley at the foot of the Atlas Mountains, the Ourika Valley is a popular daytrip for both travellers and Marrakeshi, with endless natural beauty to explore. It's especially busy in warmer months when it becomes the city's go-to escape from soaring summer temperatures.

Just an hour from Marrakesh, the Ourika Valley is a vast and scenic landscape, with tree-lined hillsides, gushing rivers and cascading waterfalls. Over the years it has fallen victim to its popularity, with increasing development, packed tour buses, makeshift riverside restaurants and barbecues, and the pollution that comes with them, which have somewhat overshadowed the valley's beauty. However, there remain unspoiled corners left to explore.

Perched at the apex of the Ourika Valley, on a rocky terracotta red butte dotted with olive trees, **Kasbah Bab Ourika** (Ourika Valley, Tnine Ourika) is a luxurious hidden eco-retreat. The ideal antidote to the dusty streets of Marrakesh, the property boasts breathtaking 360-degree views of the lush green valley and Ourika River that snakes through its rolling hills. You can stay in one of the 26 chic rooms or Kasbah Bab Ourika also welcomes day visitors to dine in its exquisite restaurant. Surrounded by endless nature to discover, the retreat offers a range of hikes through nearby mountains, you can pair one of their shorter treks (with an experienced guide, approximately two hours costs 500 MAD for two people) with lunch. Served on the picturesque garden terrace, with panoramic views of the valley and snow-capped peaks of the Atlas Mountains, lunch is a collection of Moroccan–Mediterranean dishes made with homegrown produce, like slow-cooked lamb served with potato cake and ratatouille, spicy lentil fritters and charcoal cooked beef tajine. Reservations are essential. See: kasbahbabourika.com for booking and more information.

After lunch on the way back to Marrakesh, take a small detour to the **Berber Ecomuseum** (Douar Tafza, Route de l'Ourika), a not-to-be-missed destination in the Ourika Valley. This restored Berber house and museum provides an unparalleled insight into Berber culture. Each visit here is guided by the knowledgeable guides who share a wealth of information about domestic savoir-faire (know-how) of Berber tribes, the fascinating history of utensils and objects used in everyday life, and the symbolism of Berber rugs. The museum is open daily 9.30am–7pm, entrance costs 40 MAD per person.

GETTING THERE

The best way to see the Ourika Valley following this itinerary is with a private driver. The drive takes approximately an hour each way from Marrakesh. Most riads will happily organise a driver on your behalf, expect to pay 700–1200 MAD for the round trip. Alternatively, for a similar price you can book a driver online through: morocco-private-excursions.com, they have their own valley tours so you'll need to provide them with the itinerary ahead of time.

Daytrip

THE ESSENTIALS

Whether you are a first-time visitor or you have been to Marrakesh many times, this chapter is full of practical information to assist you in navigating the Red City.

GETTING TO/FROM MARRAKESH

There is only one airport, Marrakesh Menara (RAK). When departing the city, keep in mind that the airport has an additional layer of security at the front doors. In peak season, the lines to get into the airport can be long so allow a little more time than you ordinarily would.

There are three ways to get to and from the airport: bus, taxi or transfer. There is a cash machine (ATM) in the airport, on the right side of the terminal in arrivals, and you'll need cash for buses and taxis.

Bus

The bus stop is located out the front of the airport behind the main carpark. Bus 19 runs from this stop approximately every 20 minutes between 6am and 11.30pm. Among other stops, this bus stops and leaves from the Hivernage, Jemaa el-Fnaa and Bab Doukala (an area dense with riads and boutique hotels). Return tickets can be bought on the bus with cash for 30 MAD.

Taxis

The cost of a taxi from the airport to the medina or Guéliz/Ville Nouvelle is fixed at 70 MAD. Despite the fact there is an official sign confirming the fixed price in front of the taxi rank (found across the street from arrivals), the drivers will always try to negotiate on price. You can generally get them to stick to the official price but if you do have to budge, try not to go above 100 MAD.

Make sure to have cash on you, as there are rarely EFTPOS facilities in the taxis. Small notes are ideal, as taxi drivers will often say they have no change.

Transfers

Most riads and hotels will offer to arrange a transfer to/from the airport. It is always worth asking the price and comparing it to what a taxi might cost you. Sometimes the cost is only marginally more so this may be a good alternative.

THE ESSENTIALS

GETTING AROUND MARRAKESH

The ancient walls of the medina draw the line between the old and new Marrakesh. Within the walls, taxis are not able to move around so easily, as the narrow streets are not made for cars, so you will often be dropped at the nearest point possible to your destination. Taxis cannot reach many of the riads (a traditional Moroccan house converted into guesthouses and boutique hotels) in the medina, so riads will often give you a reference point to tell your driver and send someone to collect you from there.

Once in the medina, be prepared to get around on foot. Locals use motorbikes and, while they have mostly mastered the art of zipping through crowds, there is the occasional accident so be on the lookout as you walk around.

Taxis

There are two types of taxis: petite taxis that seat three people and grand taxis for up to eight people. Unfortunately, taxis are notorious for overcharging tourists and drivers almost never turn their meter on – even when asked. Asking or negotiating on price only shows that you don't know the unspoken but universally agreed rates. For first-timers, it is best to confidently jump into a taxi, state your destination and pay the standard rates upon arrival. For non-locals, these are 30 MAD during the day and 50 MAD at night, for any destination within a 15-minute drive. This will cover moving about the medina and getting to and from Guéliz/Ville Nouvelle. For anything further, it is best to agree a price before getting in the car. In addition to refusing to turn on the meter, drivers will also often pretend that they have no change. Always make sure that you have small notes or insist on stopping in at a nearby shop to break the notes before paying.

Buses

Public transport in Marrakesh is limited however the city does operate a decent bus service. Run by a company called Alsa, buses start at 6am and finish around 10pm, depending on the route. Most of the routes run every 15 to 20 minutes but timing can be a little unreliable. A route map is available on Alsa's website, but only available in French or Arabic. A useful route to note is Bus 1 to get to Guéliz/Ville Nouvelle from Jemaa el-Fnaa (buses leave from the bus stop at the end of Jemaa el-Fnaa across from the Koutoubia Mosque, see p.87). The cost for a ticket is 4 MAD.

Bicycle

Marrakesh is a flat city, making it ideal for eager cyclists. Medina Bike, the first bike-sharing system in Africa, offers 300 bikes across 10 stations around the medina. Register for an account online at: medinabike. ma, then use your code to rent a bike from one of the stations. Prices start from 50 MAD for a day pass, which offers unlimited rides (up to three hours).

DAILY LIFE IN MARRAKESH

Starting the day

The first call for prayer is around 6am (depending on the time of year) and marks the start of the day for many. While many Marrakeshis will wake up to pray, the city doesn't come alive until much later in the day. Marrakesh is calm in the early morning and the medina, in stark contrast to the rest of the day, is eerily quiet except for the occasional sound of a bicycle passing through. By 9am, Marrakesh starts to wake up and by late morning the city is in full swing.

Call for Prayer

Five times a day the muezzin's call to prayer, the Adhan in Arabic, echoes from mosque minarets across the city. Depending on the time of year, the first call to prayer of the day, Fajr, rings through the city around 6am. Last call for prayer for the evening, Al-ichae, is heard around 8pm. Most of the city's mosques are located within the medina so if you are staying in this part of the city and not a heavy

sleeper, so be prepared for a wake-up call.

Ramadan

Ramadan is a holy month in the Islamic calendar. It is dictated by the lunar calendar, and begins and ends with the appearance of the new moon, so the dates change each year. For the last few years, Ramadan has typically fallen around April/May. For Muslims, it is a month of reflection and prayer, and one where fasting (one of the five pillars of Islam) is observed. Marrakesh runs at a slower pace during the day, shops observe shorter opening hours and the streets are generally quieter, but that doesn't mean it is off-limits for tourists. All of the major sights and restaurants typically frequented by tourists remain open. And while the days may be quieter, once the sun sets the city erupts into a hive of activity as fasters break their fast with Iftar.

Attire

There is no strict dress code but locals dress conservatively. It's important to respect the local culture so dressing modestly is recommended. Opt for trousers, below-the-knee hemlines and tops covering the shoulders. That said, in the trendy restaurants and nightclubs of the Hivernage and Guéliz/Ville Nouvelle, it's not uncommon to see a more liberal approach taken to dressing after dark.

The Essentials

THE ESSENTIALS

Dinner & drinks

Dinner is normally enjoyed later in the evening so any dinner reservations are best made for between 8.30–9.30pm. Morocco has more of a cafe culture than a drinking culture, however alcohol is widely served in hotels and in restaurants outside the medina. Finding a drink within the medina walls can be difficult due to liquor licence restrictions but it's not impossible (see La Salama, p.35). In addition, many riads will serve alcohol to their guests.

Tipping

There is no strict tipping protocol in Morocco. If you would like to tip, a good rule is to simply leave a few coins or small notes in casual establishments and in more formal restaurants, tip 10% of the bill.

Drinking water

While many locals drink the tap water, if you are not used to the water it can wreak havoc on your body. Best to stick to bottled water or take a re-usable bottle with an integrated filter system.

Language

The two official languages of Morocco are Arabic and Berber, however French is widely spoken and often thought of as the country's second language after Arabic (as Berber is only spoken by a fraction of the population). Given Marrakesh's ever-growing tourism industry, English is almost always spoken at riads, hotels and restaurants. Marrakeshis living and working in the souks or streets of the medina are great linguists. Nine times out of 10 they will speak the language of their customers and it's not uncommon to hear a mix of languages being spoken in this part of the city. Compared to other Moroccan cities, the language barrier in Marrakesh is almost non-existent and visitors can generally get around without too much trouble, except for when taking taxis – when basic Arabic and French will be helpful.

Haggling

Haggling is a national sport in Morocco and Marrakeshis have perfected the art. While some stores do have fixed prices, unless you see a sign, haggling is unquestionably expected by vendors. The practice should always be approached with a friendly attitude and a smile, remember it's more of a long match of sport rather than an aggressive sprint. Always start with pleasantries before moving to price enquiries. As a general rule, try to pay a third of the price first quoted to you.

Many of the shops in the souk sell the same type of products, so if you know that you want to buy a particular type of item, it's best to ask several vendors for a price to benchmark the price range before you start seriously shopping.

THE ESSENTIALS

Hammam etiquette

Indulging in at least one hammam (bath) is a must when in Marrakesh, however it is no surprise that the thought of being scrubbed by a stranger half-naked can be a confronting idea for many. In both private and public hammams, attendees will be naked except for underwear, so make sure you pack an appropriate pair.

In public hammams, you are required to bring all of your own supplies, including soap and your own bucket for scooping water. Private hammams operate more like spas so everything will be provided for you, however it is always best to ask about the protocol when making a reservation. The Relax chapter (see p.135) has more information on the best hammams in the city.

Heckling

While walking through the medina and the souks, you may be heckled by vendors and men in the street. Unfortunately, this comes with the medina experience. While annoying and sometimes offensive, it is mostly harmless so it's best to keep walking rather than engaging with any hecklers. Be wary of any unsolicited directions and information while moving about. It is a pastime of young boys in the medina to trick tourists with fake directions and misinformation about major sights. They may offer to lead you to your destination and they'll usually take you where you need to go, but it will come at a price, so if you accept a chaperon be prepared to give a small tip for the service.

SEASONS

Long a destination for sun-seekers, Marrakesh has blue skies and sunshine year-round. While the city boasts good weather, its rhythm is indeed impacted by the seasons. Summer marks the city's low season as scorching temperatures deter visitors and even locals flee to cooler climates. Tourists tend to flock to Marrakesh in spring and autumn and over the Christmas period, searching for respite from the European winter. That said, Marrakesh offers something for everyone, no matter the season.

Winter
December–February

Winter offers blue skies and sunshine with temperatures of 17–20°C (62–68°F) during the day, but the city can be very chilly at night when the temperatures drop to 4–7°C (39–44°F), depending on the month. Morocco is a Muslim country so it's business as usual over the Christmas period in Marrakesh and while not peak season, riad and hotel prices do spike over the holiday period.

The Essentials

THE ESSENTIALS

Spring
March–May
Together with autumn, spring is one of the best seasons to visit Marrakesh. Between March and May the weather is very pleasant, warm enough for swimming (daily temperatures sit around 30°C/86°F) but not too hot for sightseeing. Spring is one of the city's high seasons so be prepared for higher prices and busy sights.

Summer
June–August
Come June, temperatures start to rise and locals make plans to escape the city in search of cooler climates for July and August – the two hottest months that see temperatures of over 40°C/104°F. For those ready to brave the high temperatures, the summer months present an opportunity to lounge by the pool at one of the city's many riads and luxury resorts at low-season prices. For those eager to spend their days exploring and sightseeing, summer is best avoided.

Autumn
September–November
Autumn is a great time to visit Marrakesh. Between September and November there are blue skies and sunshine with temperatures dropping around late September, to 20–25°C (68–77°F), through to the end of November when the city starts to cool down again. November is traditionally the wettest month of the year so be sure to pack an umbrella.

PRACTICALITIES

Currency & cash
The Moroccan Dirham (MAD) is the official currency of Morocco and prices in this book are quoted in it. It is best to carry cash at all times. While larger shops and restaurants accept most major credit cards, there is often a surcharge. Cash machines (ATMs) and currency exchange offices can be found around the city.

The exchange rates at the airport are typically higher than elsewhere in the city, so you may be better off withdrawing money from the cash machine (ATM) found in the arrivals terminal (on the right once you've cleared immigration and customs).

It is good to notify your bank before travelling to Morocco, in case your bank puts a hold on your card, thinking it's fraudulent usage.

Public holidays
There are eight public holidays observed in Morocco:
11 January (Independence
  Manifesto Day)
1 May (Labour Day)
30 July (Throne Day)
14 August (Allegiance of
  Oued Eddahab)

20 August (Islamic New Year)
21 August (Youth Day)
6 November (Green March Day)
18 November (Independence Day).
The following Islamic holidays are also observed, however as the Islamic calendar is a lunar one, dates change each year:
24 May (Ed Al-Fitr, a four-day celebration marking the end of Ramadan)
31 July (Eid Al Adha, a three-day celebration in which sheep are sacrificed)
29 October (Prophet Muhammad's Birthday).

Maps

Locals will rarely use street names and, instead, they will use landmarks as signposts when giving directions. All major sights and most stores and restaurants have street addresses registered with main digital map applications so getting around with a phone is easy enough, in theory. Don't rely on data though as signals can be patchy in some parts of the medina, so it is best to download an offline map like maps.me before leaving your accommodation or the airport, which has reliable wi-fi (see below).

Wi-fi

While some places offer wi-fi, it is not readily available outside riads and hotels so if internet access is a high priority be sure to organise mobile data. The airport has reliable wi-fi if you need to access accommodation information or maps before venturing into the city.

Phone service

The main telecommunications providers in Morocco are MarocTelecom and Orange. At the airport between clearing customs and baggage collection, you will find both providers offering free SIM cards. You can buy credit and data from both providers, who will assist you in setting up your phone with the new SIM. Otherwise, SIM cards can be bought from local tobacco stores around the city. Depending on the provider, prices start at 5 MAD for 500MB of data and go up to 100 MAD for 10GB. For calls and texts, prices also range between 5 MAD and 100 MAD for different packages.

Photographs

Locals do not like having their photo taken and will often block their face if they see you taking a shot. Try to avoid taking photos of people, unless you have their permission.

The Essentials

THANKS

I am indebted to many people who have been instrumental in the making of this book. Thank you to the team at Hardie Grant: Melissa Kayser for entrusting me with another project, Megan Cuthbert for all your support and Alice Barker for making the editing process so seamless. To Lila, from our first meeting many years ago to this second book, I'm so grateful to have had you on this journey from the beginning.

Marrakesh would not be the same city it is today without all the people that feature in these pages. I feel fortunate to have met you all. Thank you for taking the time to show me your Marrakesh, it has been an honour to see the city through your eyes.

Alistair, I will forever cherish the memories of making this book together. It is a privilege to be your friend and an even bigger one to have had you photograph this book. Thank you for exploring Marrakesh with me, for dodging monkeys in Jemaa el-Fnaa, for the early mornings and late nights, getting lost and lost again and most of all, for being able to laugh through it all.

To my friends, near and far, thank you for always being there for me. To Jeremy, for all your love and support. To my mother, thank you for instilling in me a great sense of adventure and the belief that anything is possible. Thank you to my brother for being the ultimate example of determination and my father, for all your support. To my Lulu: you are forever in my heart. This book is for you.

Published in 2020 by Hardie Grant Travel,
a division of Hardie Grant Publishing

Hardie Grant Travel (Melbourne)
Building 1, 658 Church Street
Richmond, Victoria 3121

Hardie Grant Travel (Sydney)
Level 7, 45 Jones Street
Ultimo, NSW 2007

www.hardiegrant.com/au/travel

A catalogue record for this
Book is available from the
National Library of Australia

Marrakesh, Explore the Magic of the Red City
ISBN 9781741176698

10 9 8 7 6 5 4 3 2 1

Publisher
Melissa Kayser
Project editor
Megan Cuthbert
Editor
Alice Barker
Proofreader
Jessica Smith
Cartographer
Claire Johnston
Design
Oh Babushka
Prepress
Oh Babushka and Splitting Image Colour Studio

Printed and bound in China by LEO Paper
Products LTD.